NEW

FOLK

ART

First published and distributed by
viction:workshop ltd

viction:ary™

viction:workshop ltd
Unit C, 7/F, Seabright Plaza,
9-23 Shell Street,
North Point, Hong Kong SAR
Url: www.victionary.com
Email: we@victionary.com

- @victionworkshop
- @victionworkshop
- @victionary
- @victionary

Edited and produced by viction:ary
Creative direction by Victor Cheung
Book design by viction workshop ltd

©2023 viction workshop ltd

ISBN 978-988-75666-0-1
Printed and bound in China

CONTENTS

FOREWORD

BY Tyodi Hyojin Lee

In recent years, elements from folk art have been used in many creative projects in Korea – combined with other elements across a variety of contemporary fields such as the K-pop and dance scene to create synergy. The results of these combinations can also be found in the works of popular influencers and multinational brands.

Although the visual expressions of folk art today may be different from those of the past, I believe that its inherent meaning and symbolism should be maintained because it is a country's inheritance, identity, and influence on the rest of the world. There is also an old idiom in the Analects that extols the virtue of both reviewing the old and learning the new: "溫故知新". In a literal sense, it reflects the need for creators to understand the art of the past to create something new based on it.

In the present age, where trends are changing rapidly and cultural diversity is celebrated more than ever, folk art is easy to ignore. Many from the younger generation also believe in the stereotype that it is old-fashioned and rustic. However, the more creators we have breaking this stereotype, the more interest and respect we can cultivate for it.

In fact, there is a growing number of clever and compelling integrations of folk art with modern influences that are being well-received by people of all ages while drawing their attention to the allure of the past. Works like the visual identity for the Apple Myeongdong store, which uses the "Chaek Ga-do" motif, and DJ Peggy Gou's music video for "Starry Night" with its depictions of "Ganggang-sulae", are a testament to this.

Although the issue of cultural appropriation has popped up in recent years, I think it is possible for designers to borrow the motifs of countries other than their own. However, it is important and necessary that they deep-dive into the meaning behind the motif and the history behind its usage before borrowing it. It should never be borrowed simply because it is visually compelling or suitable for a project. This is because certain parts of history can be painful or have negative connotations, resulting in an insensitive creation.

Ultimately, the future of folk art in creativity lies in sustainability — and sustainable design is all about lasting value. As time goes by and our media sources become even more diversified, there should be a continuity of folk art, in line with the flow of modernity. After all, it would be very sad if unique stories of our culture disappeared.

To new designers looking to incorporate elements of folk art into their work, I would suggest that they always ask themselves: "Has the essence been kept?" In celebrating and perpetuating the distinct cultures from which they came through a fresh lens, the simplest formula to follow would be: Create. Share. Build a community. Repeat.

BY Marios A. Georntamilis
Founder and Head of Design at Boo Republic, Thessaloniki – Greece

06

Growing up in Greece, we saw many images of folk art and history on various aesthetic backgrounds from different eras. As we turned into young adults, we came to realise that they were in fact stories of a people, of a place.

Folk art is the informal public record of the traditional artefacts of a culture; the techniques, aesthetics, and functionality of everyday objects, filtered through traditionally available means of production. Based on this line of thinking, it was the medium from which design solutions, patterns, and materials were born – another interpretation of the famous Marshall McLuhan quote: "The medium is the message." That is to say, through repetition, these traditional artefacts have given way to the rise of artisanal production, which continues to thrive today.

As designers and illustrators, we draw inspiration and ideas from folk art – an inexhaustible source. We deconstruct compositions and reconstruct them according to our own modern-day criteria, pushing our creative boundaries to new thresholds to evolve. We filter the subject matter of folk art pieces and their original production methods in order to examine the creations holistically. In doing so, I always come to the same conclusion (perhaps for some, a generalisation) that aesthetics are inextricably linked to Mother Nature and our own existence. The interpretation of this interaction is written within folk art; for all peoples, everywhere on this planet.

In our branding work for "111Elies" handmade soaps, which is featured in this very publication, we went to museums and thoroughly researched archival materials at the "Greek Library for the Preservation of Folk Art", which is unfortunately no longer in existence. We also took an even closer look at our mothers' and grandmothers' carpets, weavings, textiles, pottery, and embroidery. Colours, materials, styles, and techniques acquire a new meaning when you look at them through the lens of creation. That's why, after revisiting and reacquainting ourselves with folk designs, illustrations, objects, and patterns, we were able to reinterpret them via new media, using current design tools and modern fonts. We also concluded that the concept of "timelessness" is ultimately innate, in all of us – like an idea, a notion, sewn with the strongest thread inside our minds and hearts.

In reality, we often pass folk art off as something touristy, outdated or kitsch. Even as professionals, we find ourselves attracted to shiny new trends or the unexplored without ever being compelled to go back to their starting points. Although one does not necessarily become a better creative by focusing on folk art, they would certainly be more fully informed and richer in the way of ideation. At the end of the day, no one really needs to re-invent the wheel. However, if one should decide to do it, it would serve them well to know the ways, methods, and ideas that preceded them. After all, someone, somewhere would have done the same.

FOREWORD

07

Comprising dots, lines, and/or shapes in a repeated or juxtaposing manner, folk art patterns are often collages derived from the culture's traditional motifs. Featuring anything from symbolic flora and fauna to distinctive geometric and graphic elements, these decorative but meaningful patterns adorned handicraft, textiles, and even architecture.

REPEATING MOTIFS AND ELEMENTS

09 — 68

PATTERN

111ELIES
SOAP BARS

111Elies or "111Olives" in Greek refers to the 111 olive trees planted by a family dedicated to natural ingredients and planet-friendly processes. In shaping the project into an ode to organic simplicity and traditional practices, Boo Republic looked to local folklore and handicraft of the past, translating several traditional Greek motifs and compositions into a new, modern visual language that reflected the products' characteristics and natural colour palette.

DESIGN
Boo Republic

CLIENT
111ELIES -
N. CHRISTOPOULOU

Q How did you decide on the particular patterns or colour schemes used in 111Elies? Are there any special meanings behind each pattern?

A We dived into the archive of 'EOMMEX' (Hellenic Organisation of Small and Medium Sized Enterprises and Handicraft), an organisation that was dedicated to collecting all folk art, across various fields of traditional production (woodcarving, carpets, textile design, pottery and more). This vast archive featured various designs used for fabric, wood, and carpets, from which we picked out designs to interpret for each soap. For example, we paired a wreath of delicate yellow flowers with our citrus and turmeric soap; and used a homey carpet design with earthy colours for our Dead Sea mud soap.

Q Could you tell us more about the traditional/folk Greek motifs in your work for 111Elies? What new elements did you incorporate into the project in order to adapt it for modern audiences?

A In order to bridge traditional motifs to the needs of contemporary packaging design, we simplified forms, made colour palettes more engaging, and digitised the illustration process. The typographical treatment features a modern marriage of sans and serif fonts, and small details like the gold foiled logotype on the top of the soap box to elevate the entire design – placing it in the contemporary sphere.

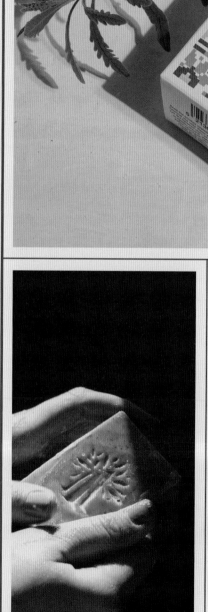

Q   Aside from health and beauty products such as 111Elies's soap bars, what other products do you think can also incorporate these unique patterns?

A   Folk art can be used successfully for many types of products that satisfy diachronic needs and allow for a connection with the past, spanning canned food, liquor, pasta, coffee, napkins, cookware, and even socks. Folk art probably would not work so well on products we correlate with "freshness", literally or figuratively, like milk or new types of snacks. The only limitations, in our humble opinion, is to be respectful to the original and have a direct connection between the product as well as its folk-related concept.

Q What part of Greek culture do you like the most? Are there any special festivals or interesting customs that you would like to share with our readers?

A Full of festivities, happiness and dancing, our culture places emphasis on enjoying the connection between humans and their hospitality. The latter is probably what we love the most – giving unconditionally and offering what you have for yourself to strangers, just to make them feel at home.

15

ΙΙΙΕLIES

HOLD ME TIGHT

DEAD SEA MUD BODY SOAP
ΣΑΠΟΥΝΙ ΣΩΜΑΤΟΣ ΜΕ ΛΑΣΠΗ ΝΕΚΡΑΣ ΘΑΛΑΣΣΑΣ

GUEREWOL FESTIVAL REBRAND

A beauty pageant with a twist, Guerewol is a colourful, centuries-old festival where men don make-up, dress up, and perform a series of enigmatic dances to attract new partners. Kenneth Kuh's rebranded identity design for the festival extends upon the tradition and rekindles the viewers' desire to liberate themselves from the burden of social stigma - even if for a brief moment.

DESIGN
Kenneth Kuh

20

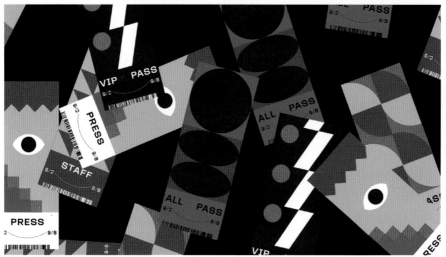

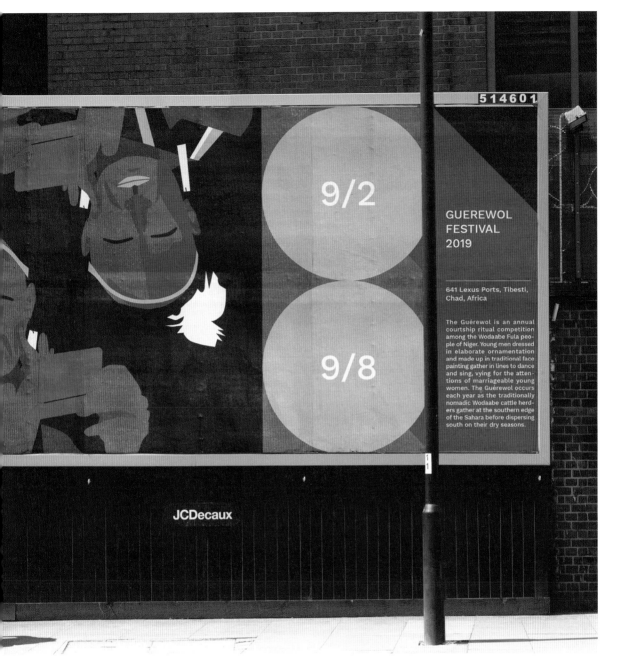

514601

9/2

9/8

GUEREWOL
FESTIVAL
2019

641 Lexus Ports, Tibesti,
Chad, Africa

The Guérewol is an annual
courtship ritual competition
among the Wodaabe Fula people of Niger. Young men dressed
in elaborate ornamentation
and made up in traditional face
painting gather in lines to dance
and sing, vying for the atten-
tions of marriageable young
women. The Guérewol occurs
each year as the traditionally
nomadic Wodaabe cattle herd-
ers gather at the southern edge
of the Sahara before dispersing
south on their dry seasons.

JCDecaux

21

HOKKAIDON

DESIGN
A Work of Substance

PHOTOGRAPHY
Vita Mak

CLIENT
1957 & C°

Hokkaidon's graphic expression is a disruption of the tranquil pattern of Seigaiha, the traditional motif of blue rolling waves. The energy of the restaurant's sea-to-table dishes unravels on the murals as the seafood breaks through, adding vigour to an ancient heritage. Rice, the foundation of Japanese food and culture, is at the core of the logo, creating a pure and distinct brand that reflects the essence of chirashi.

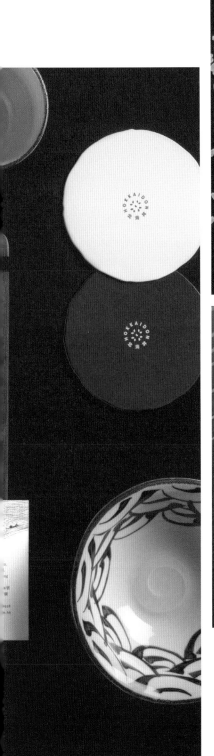

Shop 313
18 Taikoo
Taikoo Sh

香港太古
太古城中

T 2577 0828   F 2577 0928
enquiry@hokkaidon.com.hk

hokkaidon.com.hk

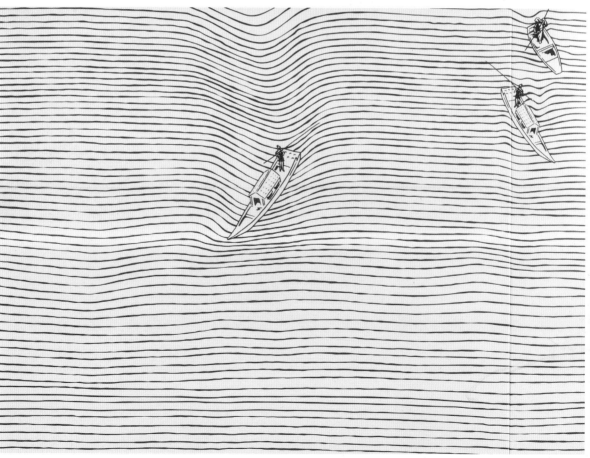

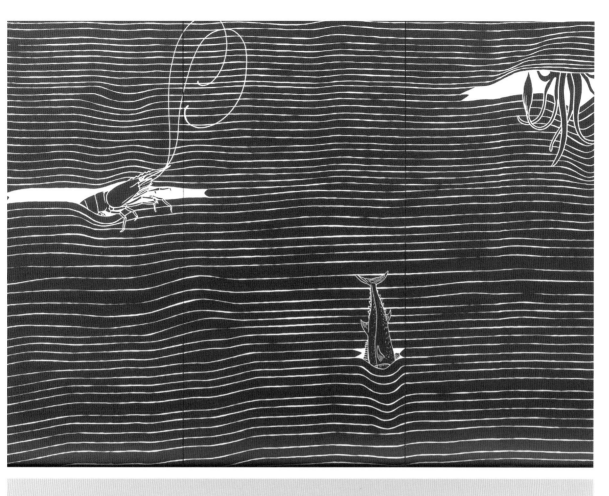

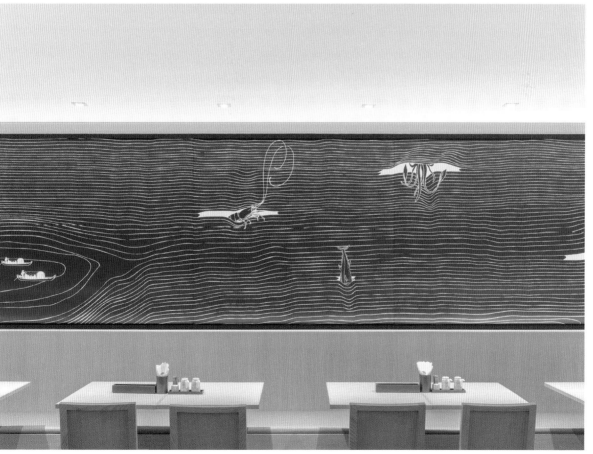

MÁXICO

Combining the words 'Mexico' and 'magic', Maxico is a travel agency that specialises in trips to Mexico's Magical Villages from abroad. Monotypo Studio was inspired by Huichol handcrafts and the repetitive patterns found in their tapestries to reflect the country's wealth of traditional culture. Máxico's icon features the eagle, a symbol of the four cardinal points and an iconic animal in pre-Columbian culture.

DESIGN
Monotypo Studio

CLIENT
Maxico Travel Agency

PHOTOGRAPHY
Diana Cristina Espinoza García

27

SUPER DELICIOUS COMPANY

Zilin Yee's work for Super Delicious Company is based on the idea of joss paper burning. According to Chinese folk beliefs, ancestors would receive 'hell money' in the afterlife if joss papers were burnt at their graves during Qing Ming or Tomb Sweeping Day. It is also said that when people burn incense and joss papers while praying, their prayers will follow the smoke to reach the souls of the dead.

DESIGN
Zilin Yee

COPYWRITING
Herbie Phoon

28

29

ONE OF TWELVE

DESIGN
ANAGRAMA

CLIENT
One of Twelve

PHOTOGRAPHY
Caroga Foto

One of Twelve is a product brand that showcases art from emerging and established Aboriginal artists in Australia. For its visual identity, ANAGRAMA drew inspiration from the lines, dots, and colours found in traditional Aboriginal art. The logotype was derived from a simple play of words and numbers that tie in with the dot system, where only one of twelve dots are coloured a bright orange.

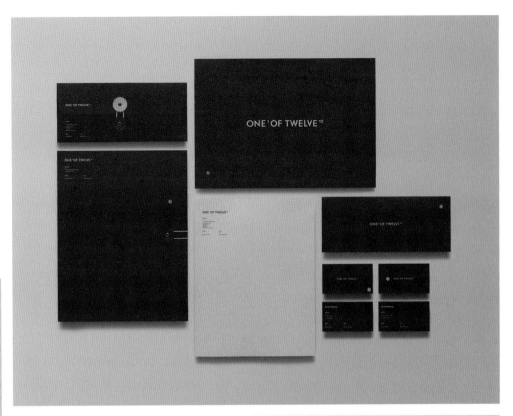

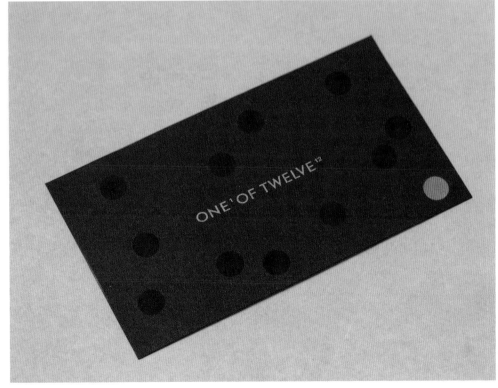

MACHIYENGA TREE TO BAR

DESIGN
Alejandro Gavancho

PHOTOGRAPHY
Sumiko Miura

CLIENT
Ivan Murrugarra

Machiyenga's name stems from the Machiguenga, an indigenous community whose ancestors inhabited Anisuyu in western Cuzco under the Incan Empire. As it would be sold mainly in Cuzco and targeted at tourists, the bean-to-bar chocolate's brand identity and packaging needed to feel intrinsicly Peruvian without falling into cliches. To that end, Alejandro Gavancho focused on creating a premium and polished modern aesthetic while preserving the mysticism of Cuzco's ancestors.

35

THE EXOTICA COLLECTION

DESIGN
Voice

CLIENT
Hugh Hamilton Wines

Vineyard owner Hugh Hamilton is passionate about the Georgian grape variety, Saperavi, as well as the region it hails from, which dates back to 6,000 BC. With the help of master Georgian winemaker Lado Uzunashvili, he released the limited edition Exotica Collection, comprising four varieties born and bred in Georgia and Australia. Its packaging was designed to intrigue wine lovers and celebrate the exclusivity of the astounding collection.

AFRIKA

DESIGN
Emi Renzi

COLLABORATOR
Typeverything

AFRIKA is a coffee brand that assembles the best beans from around the continent. Inspired by the motifs, geometric patterns, and contrasting colours found in African traditional culture, its packaging design features a flexible graphic system based on an orthogonal grid, allowing for an almost-infinite visual language with millions of outcomes that feature the different flora, fauna, and traditional patterns found within the region.

40

PAMI SNACKS

DESIGN
Monotypo Studio

CLIENT
PAMI Snacks

PHOTOGRAPHY
Diana Cristina Espinoza García

Pami Snacks creates natural food products for athletes. In designing its logo, Monotypo Studio was informed by the concept of life emerging from the earth, branching upwards as a symbol of freedom. The packaging concept was inspired by the richness of Mexican cultural traditions, namely, the folk art of the Otomi tribe and on Tonala pottery - characterised by a series of stag illustrations painted in blue watercolour.

INDONESIAN FILM FESTIVAL

The Indonesian Film Festival in Australia was established organically through annual movie screenings with different themes. Its flexible visual identity in 2016 was inspired by the subtle elements of the country's cultural visuals, which were then reworked into a generative module that could easily be reshaped into many outcomes for long-term applications and open-ended possibilities, including ever-diverse Indonesian ornaments and patterns.

DESIGN
Work by \\'

CLIENT
Indonesian Film Festival

PHOTOGRAPHY
Stephanes Mering

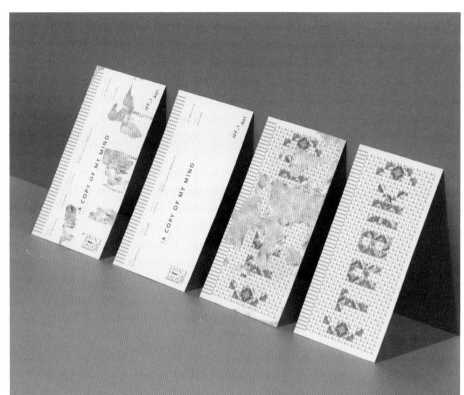

46

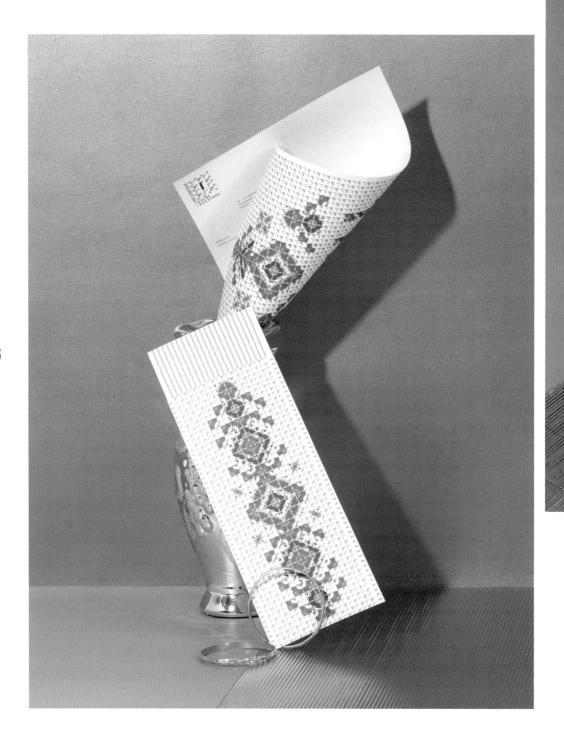

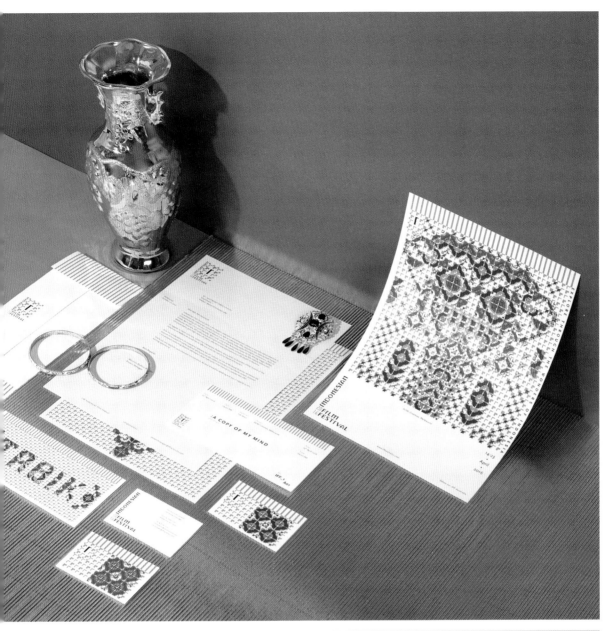

TRADITIONAL BEVERAGE

Nastya Lukina was tasked with developing the packaging design for a DIY beverage brand featuring traditional recipes and natural ingredients. In staying away from the visual solutions typically used for this product segment, she focused on images of animals found in Russian folklore and angular-style illustrations referring to woodcrafting and peasant handicrafts. The themes on the label were derived from the coats of arms of several Russian cities.

DESIGN
Nastya Lukina

ILLUSTRATION
Katia Gaigalova

CLIENT
Medovy Dom

49

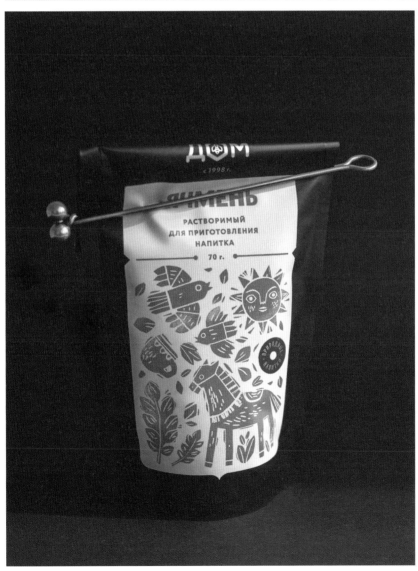

MAÜA CHOCOLATES

Maüa is a brand of craft chocolates that brings together the best of Mallorca and the tropics in terms of culture, flavour, and tradition. To represent this fusion, Barceló Estudio created a flexible pattern system by mixing Mallorcan and tropical elements such as the texture of "llengos mallorquinas". Due to the brand's wide range of products, the system allowed for a versatile and colourful visual identity.

DESIGN
Barceló Estudio

CLIENT
Maüa Chocolates

LE GUESS WHO?
2018 CAMPAIGN

The artwork for the 2018 Le Guess Who? campaign was inspired by the concept of medieval and Persian carpets depicting gardens in a flat graphic way as seen from above. Dividing his illustrations into 3 stages, Nick Liefhebber sought to feature the similarities between the ever-expanding borders of natural/manmade elements and the cultural richness one would gain from the festival itself – a celebration of creativity from around the world.

DESIGN
Nick Liefhebber

CLIENT
Le Guess Who?

THE TREASURE OF ZBOJNÍKS

Zbojnicka means "belonging to Zbojniks" – the latter being the Slovak equivalent of Robin Hood in the Middle Ages. Deemed a true treasure, Zbojnicka distillates were the main inspiration for Amoth's design work. Every element on the label, from the crossed shepherd's axes and shield decorated with traditional ornaments to the Velky Rozsutec mountain surrounded by dark forests, is significant and tells a unique story from Slovak folklore.

DESIGN
Amoth studio

ARTWORK
Robert Špecián

CLIENT
St. Nicolaus (Trade)

PHOTOGRAPHV
Jose Sabino (Sabino Studio)

HANAL PIXAN

DESIGN
Kimbal Estudio

INDUSTRIAL DESIGN
Alejandro Macías

PHOTOGRAPHY
Ricardo Torres

The HANAL PIXAN collection was inspired by the Day of the Dead celebration, one of the most complex traditions in Mexico. Fusing concepts from "food for the spirits" with a contemporary design to give each object a purer form, the laser engraving of the stripe showcases the stitchings of the Xocbichuy or traditional Mayan embroidery, which represents the traditional flowers in the shrine as a tribute to life and death.

56

NUMU

DESIGN
PUPILA

CLIENT
Carlos Reiche, Robert Buethe

For draft beer brand Numu, PUPILA studied the indigeous roots of the Chorotega as well as Guanacaste, a historical region in Costa Rica where Numu beer is produced, to create a contemporary reinterpretation of its folk art. Characterised by symmetrical shapes, geometric patterns, and earthy tones, the resulting packaging work was a successful endeavour in adding a modern twist to traditional artwork.

BRUN'KA

DESIGN
Gutsulyak.Studio

CLIENT
Ecolife

Brun'ka's organic cosmetics are made of herbs traditionally used in ancient Ukrainian beauty recipes. Ornaments typically found in the Rushnyk, an embroidered cloth with ritualistic and decorative purposes first mentioned in the 17th century, were the inspiration for the brand's visual language and used to showcase each product's exact herbal composition. Its central motif is the tree of life, a sacred Slavic symbol that stands for the universe and harmony.

61

SAUDADE

DESIGN
M&A CREATIVE AGENCY

CLIENT
Lousani

The Saudade collection by LOUSANI was inspired by the Portuguese traditional tiles that adorn buildings, streets, and alleys. Inspired by the meaning of the name itself – a common expression that alludes to the feeling of missing someone or the old times – its packaging design features traditional art with a contemporary twist, informed by the blue graphic patterns that can be found in almost every city in the country.

LECHBURG

DESIGN
nju:comunicazione

CLIENT
Lechburg Wines

PHOTOGRAPHY (PACKAGING)
Antonio Alaimo

For the visual identity of Lechburg, the first organic farm in the heart of Transylvania, nju:comunicazione was inspired by the rich history and traditions of the land. On top of reinterpreting the colourful costumes that Romanian children wear every 24th February, which is the Day of the Ancient Feast of Love, it designed a logotype by blending contrasts with custom-designed lettering, informed by the architectural lines of the Lechinta church.

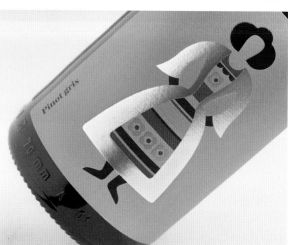

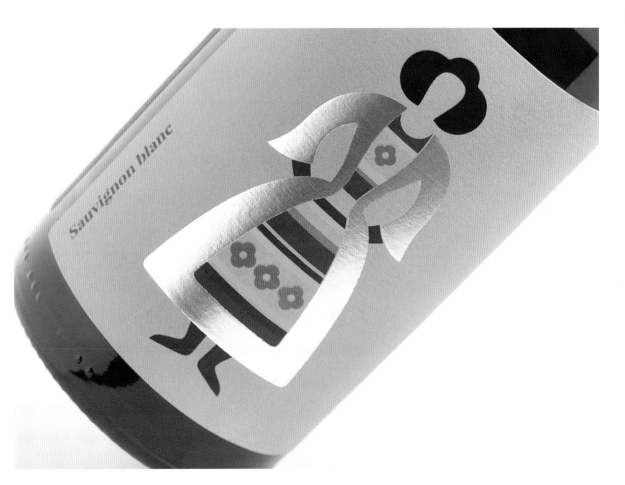

TRUEQLAB

DESIGN
Monotypo Studio

CLIENT
TrueQLab Coffee Shop

PHOTOGRAPHY
Diana Cristina Espinoza García

For coffee brand TrueQLab's packaging and identity design, Monotypo Studio aimed to showcase the best of Mexico and Colombia by fusing contemporary elements with Latin American folk culture. Besides using the deer as a motif, an animal that stands for the union of the spiritual and the material to the Wixarika tribespeople, the team also created a unique geometric pattern by reflecting the union of opposites via the coffee bean.

66

WHY WAS FOLK ART A POINT OF INSPIRATION FOR YOUR PROJECT(S)?

For us designers, folk art is a great source of inspiration because it provides the resources for creating timeless design. It is an opportunity for us to preserve and continue a story. Fusing folk art aesthetics with a contemporary approach, is what brings these stories to the present by presenting a language that can pass traditional values on to the next generations as a simple and concise message.

● Luminous Design Group

Culture is part of the product you are trying to sell; and attractive yet meaningful design is fundamental in creating a 'hook' that draws consumers to a brand. As folklore forms the root of Maua's products and their origin, we decided to give it greater visual prominence.

● Barcelo Estudio

We believe that folk art is found everywhere in Mexico; it is part of our culture and our history. Death in Mexico is a representation and commemoration of those who are no longer with us; a party that is celebrated in different parts of the country.

● HI! ESTUDIO

Before I started working on this project, I had come across an exhibition on Buddhist paintings from the Goryeo dynasty in Korea. Through the exhibits, I saw the delicate beauty of Buddha through different elements of the paintings that contained different meanings. As a result, I strived to reinterpret a Buddhist painting in my own style some day – leading to the 'Dangun Paper Theatre'.

● Dasom Yun

This project was directly inspired by one of the traditions deeply rooted in Mexican culture: the Day of the Dead. Our country has always had an iconographic wealth that is reflected in our clothing and kitchen utensils – important parts of everyday life. The combination of embroidered art translated into daily tools was used to achieve a unique image that feels like part of our traditional graphic language.

● Kimbal Estudio

As someone who has always been fascinated by art and culture, I am particularly taken by decorative art, especially folk art that is bright, lively, and at times naive. I am also a big fan of mid-century modernist, industrial, and print designs that celebrate conciseness and the wit of solutions through stylish minimalism. When I decided to produce items of my own design, I did not want to bring them to life at some factory, but rather, keep up with traditions in the production process - which is why we turned to the masters of Russian artisanal souvenirs for help. It has been challenging at times but always rewarding so far!

● Kseniia Shishkova

The Zbojnicka project was initially focused on folklore. Distillates in Slovakia were traditionally consumed as folk drinks and the Zbojniks were prototypes of local folk in their purest form. In ancient times, the most courageous people were fighting for their rights and justice for ordinary people, farmers, and shepherds. At the intersection of these two facts, a series of distillates was born under the name Zbojnicka, which means 'belonging to Zbojniks'. Appropriating the right visualisation was necessary for a product with such a high concentration of themes. Therefore, we turned to traditional Slovak visuals, creating a story for the label by referring to images and symbols from the Zbojniks era. We also used ornaments from different regions in Slovakia for authenticity. Overall, the work refers to the past and yet, transcends time.

● Amoth studio

For this project, the location and the brand needed to clearly be 'of place'. That meant looking into the long history of Kilmartin in great detail. We focused on organising the information and making sense of it all, before communicating the aesthetics in a way that they sympathised with the identity and packaging design.

● My Creative

Since ancient times, people have gone to temples to worship the gods and pray for peace and prosperity. There are many rituals involved upon each visit, such as making offerings, burning incense for blessings, and making robes for the gods. The most distinctive of these is the pattern and embroidery on the gods' robes, the technique for which is very important for making the garments stronger and more beautiful. However, hand-made embroidery is gradually being replaced by machines today, with less and less people understanding this traditional artform.

● Yufang Wang

Folk art was the main inspiration for this project because we felt the necessity to use historic graphics and recreate/reinterpret them through a modern lens to allow more people to learn and connect with the culture. It was really important for us to respect the original art that was taken as inspiration, so we crafted every detail, including the fonts, logotype, and patterns very carefully to convey the same message but with our added creative input.

● Alejandro Gavancho

I have always been attracted to different ethnic groups from different countries – the cultures that are lived and breathed in different parts of the world and throughout history. Within each of these cultural roots, we can find a surprising aesthetic richness, whether it be through clothing, music/instruments or customs, among many other things. It fuels my passion to create art or products with a powerful concept.

● Emi Renzi

Toyohashi City in the Aichi prefecture is known as the production centre of a traditional Japanese apron called 'maekake'. After World War II, the city saw a rapid increase in maekake production as demand increased. Today, however, only one factory remains – and it continues to weave the thick maekake fabric called 'ichi-go' which has been used since the Edo period. The maekake culture and industry – a symbol of Japanese merchant culture – can almost be said to be a dying industry. In rebranding the aprons made by this last factory in Japan, we thought about creating a packaging design that could compete in the current market while expressing the historical background of the product.

● NOSIGNER / Eisuke Tachikawa

As Chinese-Malaysians, we have always found Chinese culture and folk art interesting. Typically, folk art items can still be found in Chinese homes today – but are often neglected. The level of understanding for these items is relatively low.

● Where's Gut Studio

This entire project was inspired by local culture. In Sicily, there is an amazing heritage of art, food, architecture, and music – and within each field, you will find some amazing local traditions. In this case, our starting point was the 'Pupi Siciliani', the ancient tradition of making puppets.

● Happycentro

To develop the concept for this project, I looked for a narrative that the festival could be based on. The artwork is inspired by the concept of medieval and Persian carpets depicting gardens in a flat graphic way as seen from above – showing ever-expanding borders of lush greenery, fountains, and architecture just as the festival showcases the richness of the music and arts scene worldwide. The poster was revealed in three stages, beginning at the centre or the festival itself and zooming out to reveal more artists and art every step of the way.

● Nick Liefhebber

As the company (TrueQLab) was built on the hard work of a Mexican and a Colombian living abroad, we sought to create a visual identity that reflected the best of both cultures. We looked to the Latin American artisan culture for inspiration, as we believe that Latin artisanal traditions should be promoted internationally.

● Monotypo Studio

Folk art is an inseparable part of daily culture. To start a new dialogue through my work, I pay tribute to its traditional qualities and techniques through modern expressions. The viewer should be able to sense the interweaving of the past and the present, as if opening a time capsule.

● ZISHI

We delved deeply into Armenian folk traditions, extracting the most unique ones and presenting them with a modern twist to complete the restaurant's vibrant atmosphere. Hand-drawn illustrations, manuscripts, and calligraphies depicting famous toasts, feasting culture, and wine-drinking can all be found on the bottle wrappers. We found this to be the best way to demonstrate that traditions and folk art can stay relevant in the modern world.

● Backbone Branding

This project was created as a solution to the problem where barefooted children in Bangladesh often get injured and even lose their lives from wounds caused by lying debris and glass. TEKITOJUKU learnt that a shoe manufacturer was working to produce and sell inexpensive shoes, and decided to collaborate with them in creating footwear that anyone could afford. Waraji is a Japanese craft from Akita Prefecture where straw sandals can be made with even a low budget. Therefore, we learnt the technique from local Akita craftsmen, and passed them onto Bangladesh.

● TEKITOJUKU

Not only is the Ox the protagonist for 2021 in the Chinese calendar, it is also a highly valued animal in agriculture admired for its diligence, integrity, and honesty. The relationship between the Ox and humans has been strong throughout history, and as folk art reflects the cultural life of a community, we found the 'Ge Ba' to be the perfect conduit to bridge the two elements together.

● A Work of Substance

The rich fauna and mystic aura of Oaxaca were the main inspiration for the brand, so we revisited traditional alebrijes of the region and elevated them with a contemporary take for a global audience, inspired by Guadalupe Posada's etchings. Alebrijes are woodcrafted creations made from various animals, merged into one. As mezcal is mostly made in Oaxaca, we wanted this folk inspiration reflected on each of the mezcal expressions and its labels.

● Menta.

Greek – in particular, 17th-century Cretan – culture influenced the whole concept for this project. Besides deriving the black and terracotta colour palette from ancient Greek pottery and ceramic artefacts, we did a lot of research on Greek fonts of the era, which were originally created by Italian foundries out of Latin alphabet print elements. The casting of the Greek letters led to a visually interesting and unique font system, due to the assymetrical design elements, small defects of the casts, and intonation. Overall, our choices sought to unify the concept and solidify the essence of the historical period.

● Boo Republic

We typically conduct an in-depth study on our client and the territory before starting on a specific design project. In this case, folk art was relevant for showcasing the roots of the people who make wine in the land of Transylvania.

● nju:comunicazione

The Brun'ka brand is bound to Ukrainian heritage and brings authentic local beauty recipes to life. It bridges ancient knowledge about nature that is integral to folklore with the modern beauty industry, which is why folk art became the most valuable and relevant inspiration source for this project – a dichotomy of folk rituals and spa treatments, as well as pagan beliefs and science.

● Gutsulyak.Studio

The Hikiyama Festival has had a long history in Nagahama City in the Shiga prefecture and is famous for its special kabuki performance by children on the day. As it has been registered as a UNESCO Intangible Cultural Heritage, I based my design on the idea of spreading this culture like a package of sweets.

● Masahiro Minami Design

In a highly homogenised world, it is very important to be able to stand out from other companies that offer the same services. For this reason, we wanted to create a brand that transmitted the values of the company effectively – and more so, for one focused on promoting trips to Mexico from abroad. We used the Wixarika (Huichol) culture and prehispanic traditions as a starting point, and added a modern, elegant, and sophisticated touch to show the magic of Mexico to the world.

● Monotypo Studio

The whole idea behind the company's name was inspired by Chorotega culture, especially since Numu is based in the area where the Chorotegas used to inhabit. As such, we looked to the people, their art, and history for inspiration.

● PUPILA

In Chinese culture, 'xian-grui' or patterns of auspicious flora and fauna including fish and butterflies often appear on hand-painted characters on couplets and colourful paper-cuttings during the Chinese Spring Festival. In recent years, I noticed how these decorations have been over-simplified or exaggerated, and decided to create a new interpretation of these hand-painted characters and patterns while maintaining their cultural roots. By combining 'xian-grui' patterns with a minimal background, I wanted to add a playful touch to the coffee packaging that did not forgo the traditional elements that reminded viewers of the rich cultural context behind the festival.

● Lung-Hao Chiang

Folk art is typically made by craftsmen during a specific time period within a specific cultural context. It contains the stories and memories of the past. By incorporating folk art elements, we can add new layers of storytelling into our designs.

● Onion Design Associates

A single object can carry many different meanings. Whether it is the skull that represents death and rebirth in Mexican tradition or the turtles and cranes that represent longevity in Korea, these animate and inanimate symbols are typically used to convey deeper messages in art and design.

69 — 134

SYMBOL

MEANINGFUL
REPRESENTATIVE
SYMBOLS

SIPJANG-SAENG: Korean Ten Symbols of Longevity

In the olden days, Korean elders were known to keep several objects symbolising perennial youth and longevity by their side, also known as <SIPJANG-SAENG: Korean Ten Symbols of Longevity>. Although the fundamental human desire to live forever has not changed, people today simply focus on how to live a long and healthy life. TUKATA® TRADITIONAL's take on the original symbols deliver traditional Korean wisdom and values through a fresh perspective.

DESIGN
TUKATA

PHOTOGRAPHV
Garam Jeon, Soosoo Jang

Q   We noticed that each of the seven
    symbols of longevity by TUKATA has
    a distinct face that adds a touch of
    humour and cuteness to the products.
    What was the reason behind this par-
    ticular decision?

A   TUKATA TRADITIONAL is a project inspired by
    the ancient Korean concept of 'Ten Symbols of
    Longevity'. Using the motifs of the 10 symbols
    as inspiration, we developed various charac-
    ters and lifestyle items that feature a unique
    expression that is also an element of TUKA-
    TA's brand identity. If you look closely at their
    expressions, they appear to be slightly angry.
    This was inspired by 'Jangseung', a traditional
    Korean element. Moreover, this was done
    to reflect the strong and dignified image of
    our ancestors.

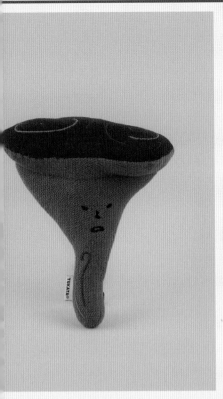

Q   Besides pins, toys, and fabrics, are there any more products that you are interested in making for TUKATA?

A   We are always thinking about sustainability. So, we plan to develop recycled products using scrap fabric to contribute to improving the global environment. We believe that even if we use scrap fabric, there will be enough cute and lovely things.

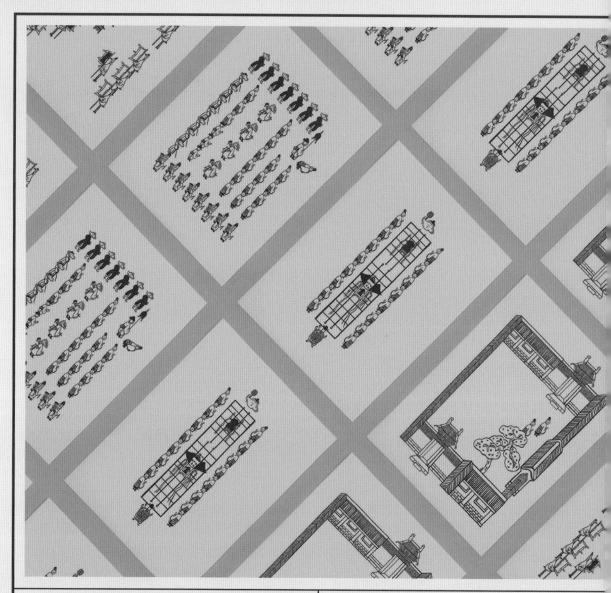

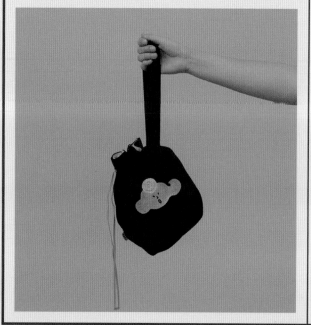

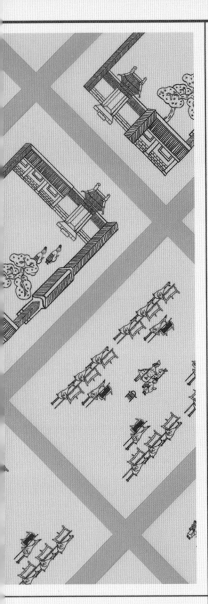

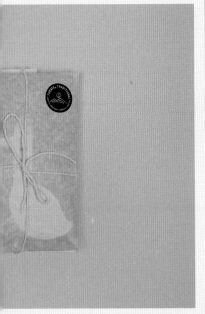

Q With the rise of Hallyu (Korean wave) via K-Pop, K-dramas, and movies in recent years, South Korea has swept the world with the influence of its soft power. What more do you think can be done to promote South Korea's traditional culture?

A TUKATA will continue to maintain the TUKATA TRADITIONAL lineup to promote Korean traditional culture, and develop various items that utilise traditional Korean elements in addition to the 'Ten Symbols of Longevity'.

Q What part of Korean culture do you like the most? Are there any special festivals or interesting customs that you would like to share with our readers?

A We like how Korea is beginning to embrace diverse cultures and becoming more open. We believe that Korea has the advantage of rapidly absorbing various cultures and changing trends. One interesting festival is Hanbok Culture Week which is held every October in Korea to celebrate our country's traditional clothing, the Hanbok. Participants can experience hands-on events related to Hanbok from all over the country.

75

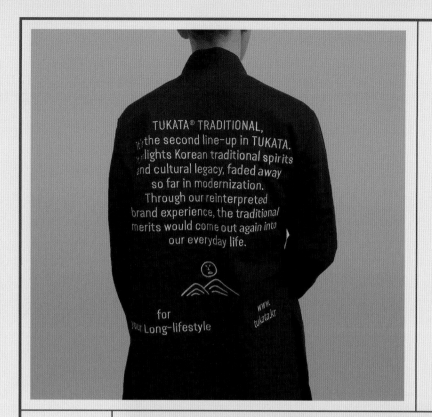

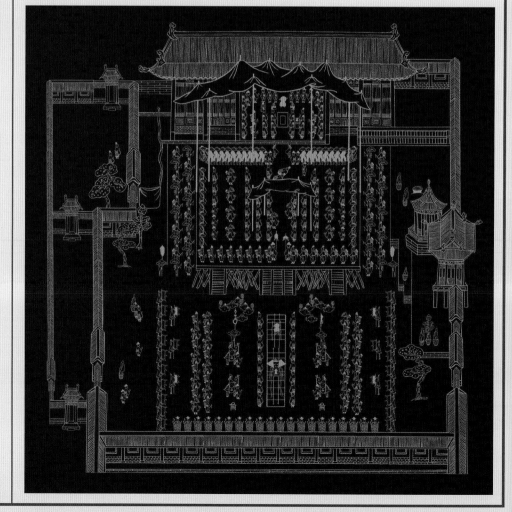

KABUKI KIDS

DESIGN
Masahiro Minami Design

CLIENT
Kasho Rokube

Masahiro Minami Design's packaging work for KABUKI KIDS honours the traditions of the Hikiyama Matsuri, a traditional float festival in Nagahama which began 400 years ago in the Azuchi Momoyama era and is famous for its special kabuki performance by children. The specially-designed box that playfully turns into a kabuki mask also commemorates the addition of the festival to UNESCO's registry of Intangible Cultural Heritage of Humanity registry in 2016.

79

SCENTS OF DAO

DESIGN
A Work of Substance

PHOTOGRAPHY
Vita Mak, Judy Chen

Scents of Dao was formed to translate the ancient teachings of Shen Nong, the father of Eastern herbal medicine, into modern-day contexts. In crafting them into a precise methodical philosophy centred around the body's balance and energy systems, the brand unites elements of the Sun and Moon – characterised by merging their two Chinese symbols – to become an anchor for harmonious day-to-night rituals.

TEQUILA SOLEDAD DÍA DE MUERTOS EDITION

Inspired by artist Efren Gonzalez's painting on the Wall of the Dead in Ajijic, as well as the concept of death, traditions, and those no longer in the world, Hi! Estudio paid homage to ancient Mexican customs and heritage with limited-edition Day of the Dead packaging and bottle designs for Tequila Soledad. Each bottle was embellished with skull motifs and came with a bespoke skull charm.

DESIGN
HI! ESTUDIO

PHOTOGRAPHY
HI! ESTUDIO, Mariel Miranda

CLIENT
I & A AGAVE SPIRITS

84

IZUMO TAISHA SAITAMA BRANCH

DESIGN
6D

CLIENT
Izumo Taisha Shrine,
Saitama Branch

CREATIVE DIRECTION
Vu Vamada / method

ILLUSTRATION
Hiroki Taniguchi

6D was tasked with rebranding the Saitama branch of Izumo Taisha, a revered shrine where gods were believed to gather. The studio designed a new coat of arms that combined the shrine's emblem, a hexagon with a tortoise-shell pattern, and the clouds of Izumo. Various applications were also created based on the emblem, including kites and amulets that featured traditional lucky motifs such as rabbits, turtles, and cranes.

86

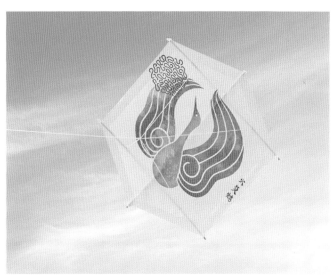

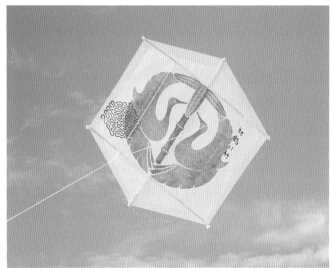

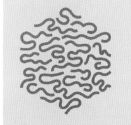

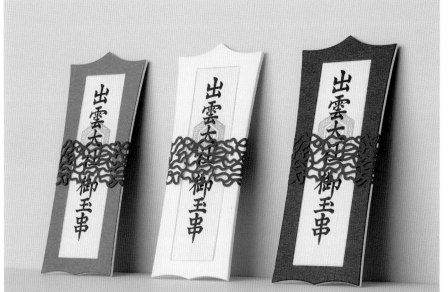

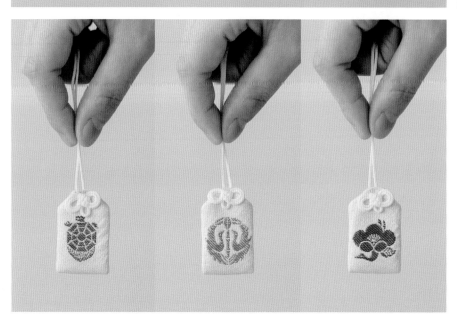

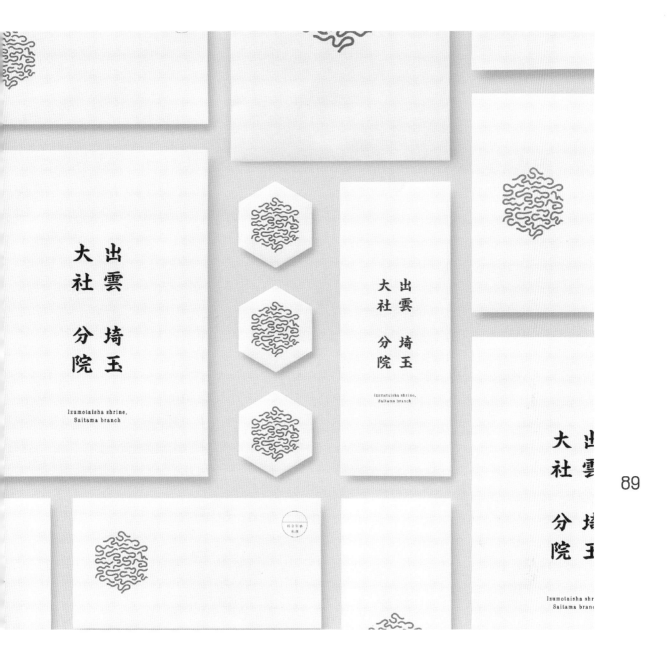

参拝方法　二拝 四拍手 一拝

お賽銭を入れ、お願い事をします

次に──────一拝

──────二拝　深いお辞儀を二度行います

出雲大社　縁むすび　家内安全　厄除
　　　　　病気平癒　学業成就
祖霊社　　幽世（あの世）を治めている神様

91

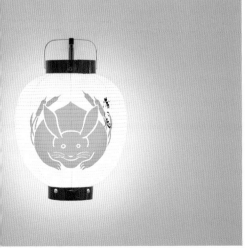

LEGEND OF
THE FIVE TIGERS

Like a mysterious jungle filled with wonder, the post-pandemic world is brimming with both uncertainties and opportunities. At the centre of the jungle are the Five Tigers, the strategic and swift beasts featured in B&A Studio's Lunar New Year gift set. Inspired by Hang Trong folk woodcut paintings, the small boxes contain gifts of traditional Vietnamese fine crafts and cuisine.

DESIGN
B&A Studio

ILLUSTRATION
Kris Nguyen

CLIENT
SPG Invest

PHOTOGRAPHY
Fuongy Nguyen

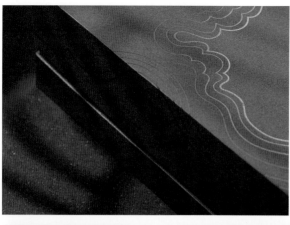
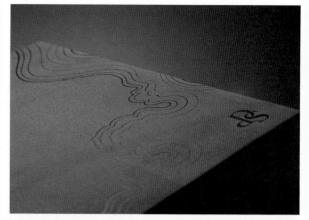

OEVOTAS
OLIVE OIL

DESIGN
Ioannis Fetanis

CLIENT
Nikolaos Apostolopoulos

PHOTOGRAPHY
Christos Kotsinis

BOTTLE DECORATION
Print on Glass

Oevotas Elixir olive oil products are derived from two olive species exclusively cultivated in the west of the Peloponnese Peninsula. Besides paying tribute to the runner Oevotas who won the 6th Olympics in 756 B.C., the brand's design approach is also rooted in Greek folklore elements with obvious archaic influences in typography. Its ceramic vessel was also inspired by "lekythos", a type of Greek pottery in ancient times.

MỘT NÉN TÂM HƯƠNG INCENSE PACKAGING

The burning of incense has long been a Vietnamese custom and is a familiar sight throughout the country. However, most of the incense brands in the market today are lacking in terms of packaging aesthetics. Inspired by his own family's rituals and the four mythical creatures in Vietnamese culture, motchutmy set out to elevate the image of the everyday product from a fresh design perspective.

DESIGN
motchutmy, Ngoc Thao

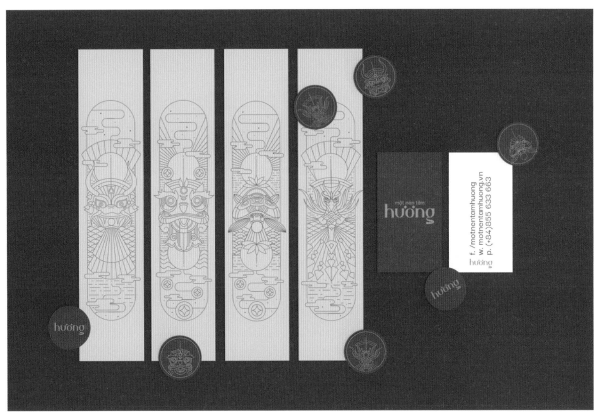

KILMARTIN GIN

DESIGN
My Creative

CLIENT
Kilmartin Glen Spirits

As one of Scotland's richest pre-historic landscapes, Kilmartin Glen is of profound significance to its people, spanning 5,000 years. My Creative's work for Kilmartin Gin took influence from the rock carvings left by the first people, whose creativity and craft can still be seen today. By reimagining their culture and its symbolism, the studio reflected the heritage and quality of the product in a modern and refined way.

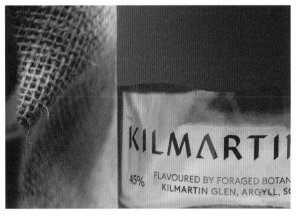

KIM KHÁNH – TRADITIONAL BAKERY

Kim Khánh is a traditional Vietnamese bakery that was established in the 1960s. Famous for its cakes that have preserved their original flavours from the past, it wanted to preserve the bakery's heritage itself through a modern and distinctive brand identity. To that end, Quang Bao designed an illustrative and flexible logo derived from Eastern folklore to not only evoke the essence of tradition, but to also appeal to today's audiences.

DESIGN
Quang Bao

CLIENT
Kim Khánh

PHOTOGRAPHY
Jade Le

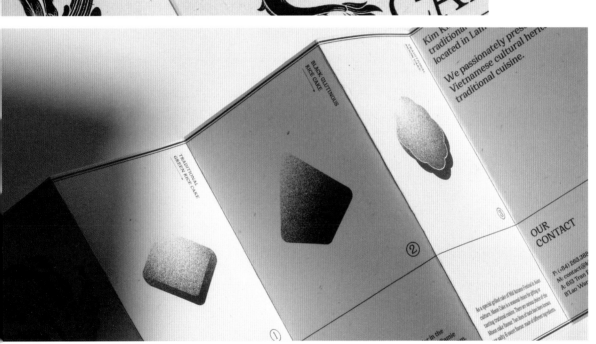

1821–2021: FEELING OUT THE NATIONAL SELF

For the visual identity and exhibition graphics of '1821-2021: FEELING OUT the NATIONAL SELF', Studio Hervik created a series of 'faces' representing the Greek national consciousness and memories of 1821, underlined by a mood of introspection and critical evaluation. Derived from folk art, shadow theatre as well as anonymous figures and anthropocentric compositions in wood-carved objects, the work combined unique typography with historical markings and a folk-inspired colour palette.

DESIGN
Studio Hervik

CLIENT
Ministry of Culture and Sports,
Folklife and Ethnological Museum of
Macedonia – Thrace

104

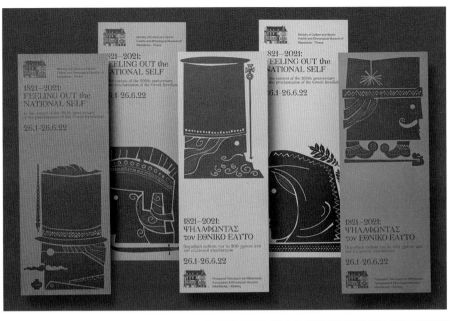

ANYTHING

DESIGN
NOSIGNER / Eisuke Tachikawa

CLIENT
Anything C⁰, Ltd

Maekake are Japanese workclothes wrapped around the waist like an apron, used mainly in liquor, fish, and rice stores. For Anything, a brand created with the craftsmen of the last 'ichi-gō' maekake manufacturing factory, NOS-IGNER updated the product's image by printing the design of a miniature maekake on top of a pair of illustrated legs on rice bags to convey the brand's diverse lineup and how maekake should be worn.

THE LOST EXPLORER MEZCAL

The Lost Explorer is an artisanal handcrafted mezcal made from agave cultivated in the sun-soaked Valles Centrales of Oaxaca. Inspired by the spirit of the brand that celebrates the earth as well as the diversity and wonder of the sacred plant, Menta. revisited traditional alebrijes of the region and elevated them for a global audience with a contemporary take inspired by Guadalupe Posada's etchings.

DESIGN
Menta.

CLIENT
David de Rothschild,
Thor Björgólfsson

ILLUSTRATION
Daniel Barba

PHOTOGRAPHY
Frica, Lily Wan

109

HANBOK CULTURE WEEK

HANBOK CULTURE WEEK sets out to cultivate public interest in the traditional Korean clothing by promoting its industrial and cultural values on a global scale. Originally a single-day event that was held since 1997, it suffered from an inconsistent, often-outdated visual identity, tone and manner until it took on its current format in 2018. Today, it boasts a refreshed look that helps the hanbok break away from its stereotypical image.

DESIGN
Tyodi Hyojin Lee

SUPERVISION
KOREA Ministry of Culture, Sports and Tourism,
KOREA Craft & Design Foundation,
Hanbok Advanced Center

BX DESIGN
Tyodi Hyojin Lee, Hyunwoo Kim

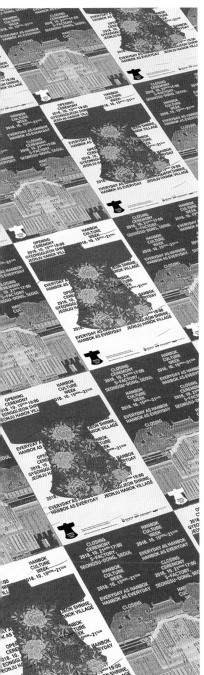

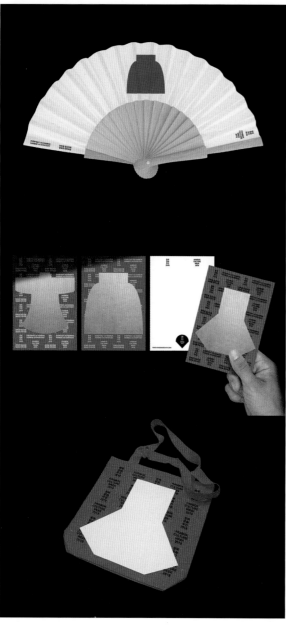

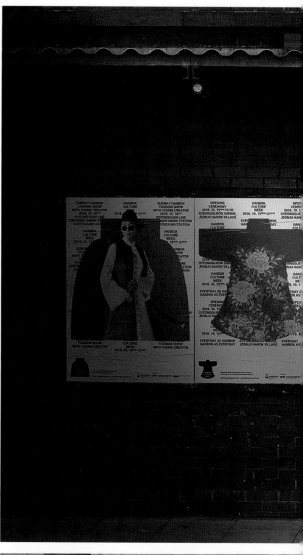

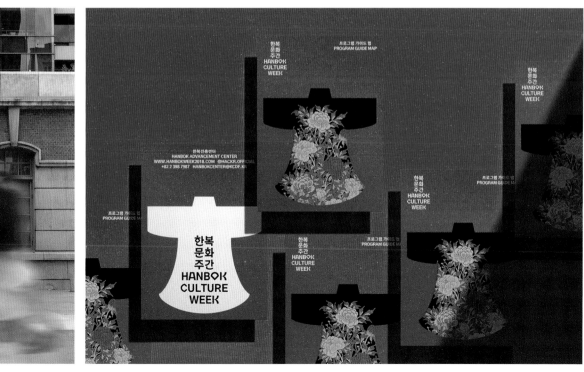

SKOUTARI OLIVE OIL

"Shield" in the Cretan dialect, Skoutari was borrowed from Vincenzo Cornaro's epic "Erotokritos", in which it was used to protect the protagonist in a jousting that takes place to impress his beloved – just as olive oil protects the human body. Horses were featured as an indirect reference to the literary text, whereas the linocut technique and colour of the bottle were inspired by ancient Greek pottery and artefacts.

DESIGN
Boo Republic

PHOTOGRAPHY
Stefanos Tsakiris

CLIENT
The Vardas Family

GREAT YEAR

DESIGN
Lung-Hao Chiang

In creating the packaging design for 'Great Year' coffee, Lung Hao-Chiang used the hand-painted characters found on couplets and paper cutting handicrafts made during Chinese New Year. Traditional auspicious patterns such as the butterfly, crane, gourds, fish, and lotus were combined with the coffee flavours. For example, the butterfly, which symbolises longevity, was paired with the honey-treated flowers and fruity taste of the coffee.

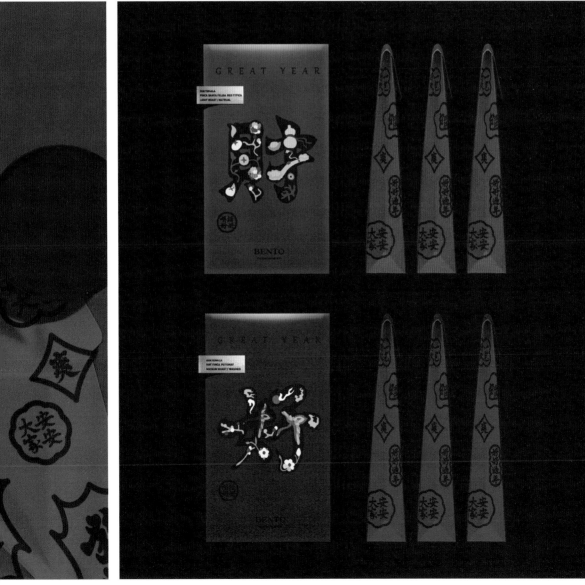

121

EBIYA

DESIGN
6D

CLIENT
Ebiya

CREATIVE DIRECTION
Yu Yamada / method

AGENCY PRODUCTION
Kiyotaka Ushikawa /
Nakagawa Masashichi Shoten

ARCHITECTURE
Takashi Kobayashi, Mana Kobayashi /
Design Office IMA

PHOTOGRAPHY
Shingo Fujimoto / sinca

Located adjacent to the revered Ise Shrine, Ebiya is a souvenir shop and cafeteria that has been in business for over 100 years. To help it rebrand and thrive into the next century, 6D designed a series of colourful pictograms using a traditional Japanese colour-grading method called 'rinpa' to depict Ise's symbolic motifs such as the torii shrine gates and local produce like beef, shrimp, and tea leaves.

122

名物
伊勢
うどん

ゑびや

二人前
たれ付き

124

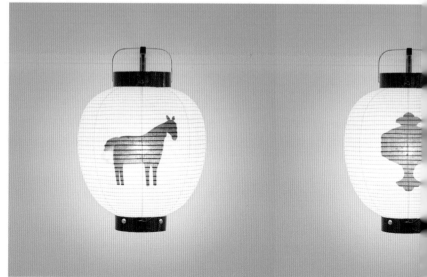

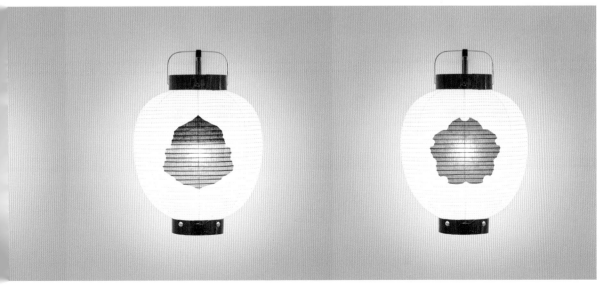

MEXICA BREWERY

Cerveceria Mexicana is one of California's first craft breweries that celebrates the diversity of Mexican culture. For its mural, Franko Ro painted a large Mexican skull alongside the Winged Serpent, which was regarded as the giver of life in prehispanic civilisations. Below the illustration, he also left a series of red and blue circles for visitors to paint their own interpretations of a skull.

DESIGN
Franko Ro

PHOTOGRAPHY
Franko Ro, Mariel Miranda

CLIENT
Cervecería Mexicana

126

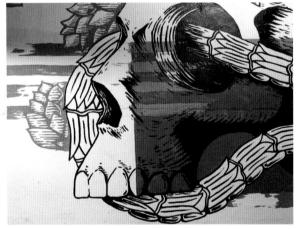

ALL GOOD SPRINGS

DESIGN
Alex Dang

The All Good Springs lucky envelope design project was based on the idea of adding a fresh element to cheerful Vietnam Tet traditions. Besides featuring familiar imagery derived from Bat Trang ceramic flower vases to evoke a nostalgic feel, Alex Dang was also inspired by folk paintings – reproducing the symbolic four prosperity trees ('Tùng Cúc Trúc Mai') via a minimal aesthetic paired with colourful tints.

130

131

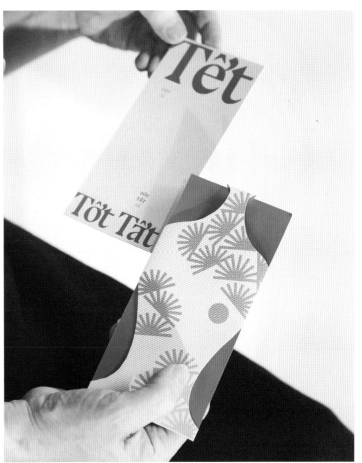

ARGENTO

DESIGN
the branding people

CLIENT
Argento

Argento is a family-owned mezcal with a century-old history. To reflect the mezcal's sustainable practices and pesticide-free plantations that allow farmers to be kinder to the land, the branding people drew inspiration from the estates located in Guerrero, an area rich with culture and folklore. The textures and patterns were informed by the evident Afro-Latin American influence within the area, with a nod to endemic elements.

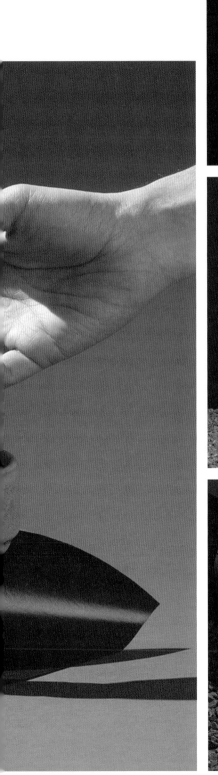

TALE

135 — 204

Stemming from age-old stories, myths, legends, and folklore that have been passed along the generations, folk tales retrace the roots of a culture through compelling narratives. In art and design, the tales are often depicted by incorporating visuals or graphic elements inspired by certain customs or festivals.

DIALOGUE WITH A WORK OF SUBSTANCE

THE YEAR OF OX

For the Year of the Ox, an animal admired for its indispensable role in Chinese agricultural society as well as its diligence and integrity, A Work of Substance designed five red packets to honour the five grains in ancient China: wheat, broomcorn, rice, foxtail millet, and soybean. Wrapped in packaging that embodies the Ox itself, the packets were also compiled into a blizzard book mechanism that carries stories within.

DESIGN
A Work of Substance

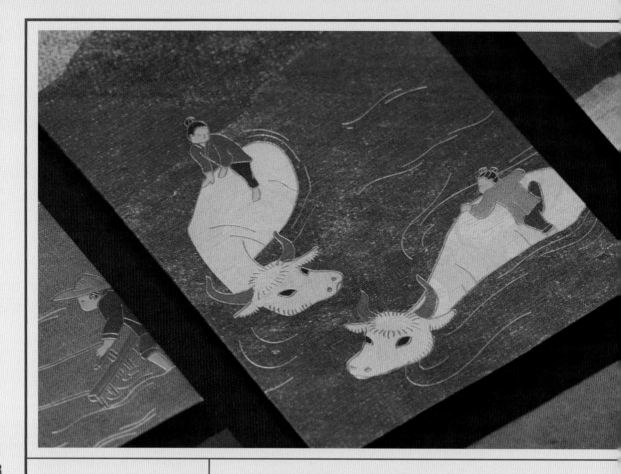

Q What was the creative decision behind using Ge Ba, the traditional textile artform as the illustrations for the red packets?

A An obscure artform found deep in the farms of China's countryside, the Ge Ba is a rare and little-known part of Chinese culture. Silk, hemp, ramie, and cotton are assembled together with rice glue, creating a piece reminiscent of a cubist painting. These collages were never appreciated at the imperial palace, and their existence is ephemeral - fabricated as quickly as they disappear. They are rarely kept, and hardly known by others except the natives themselves. Not only did we want to shed light on this unassuming craft, the Ge Ba featured are from the personal collection of François Dautresme, a prolific art collector who amassed over 7,500 items during his 35 years of travel, exploration, and discovery in China. More notably, François was also the beloved and inspiring uncle of our founder Maxime Dautresme.

Q   After creating a set of red packets
for the Year of the Ox, would you con-
sider creating a set for each animal
in the Chinese zodiac in later years?

A   We design a set of red packets every Chinese New
Year, allowing us to uncover distinctive stories
and craft creative ways to celebrate the Zodiac
animal of that year.

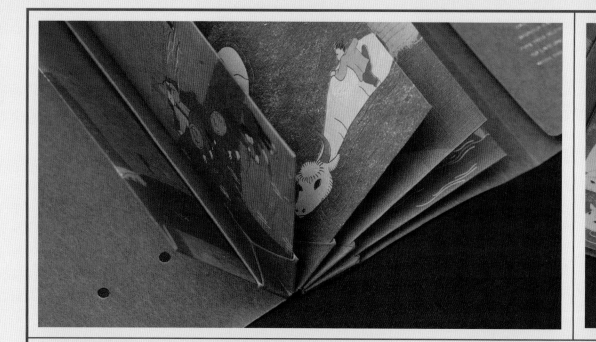

Q With the trend of electronic red packets on the rise due to convenience and environmental concerns, do you think there is still a demand for paper red packets today?

A Certainly. At Substance, we do not believe in only the digital world. There is so much to discover and experience in the physical world, and there's room to find innovative ways to re- use, re-purpose, and sustain.

Q What part of Chinese culture do you like the most? Are there any special festivals or interesting customs that you would like to share with our readers?

A We would love to share the Chinese approach to arts and craft, or as described by Francois Dautresme, "the natural chain of what man can produce if he is respectful of his past, with its extraordinary manual dexterity and possessed by the rhythms of nature."

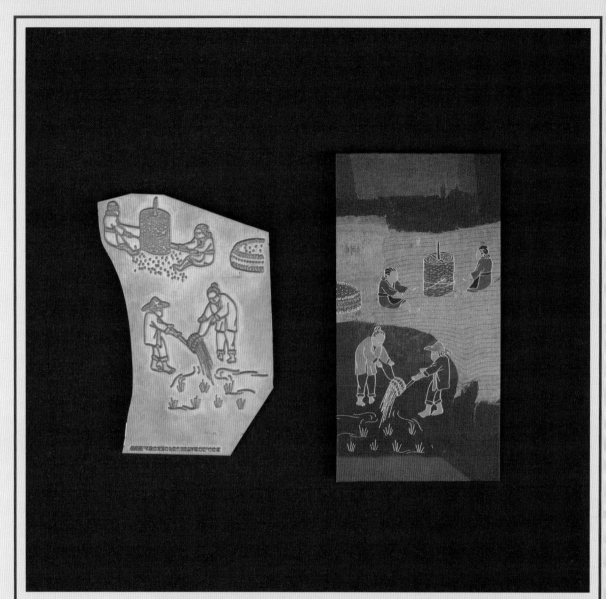

UKIYO-E CHOCOLATE

Vsevolod's packaging design for a limited-collection series of chocolates that was created for the State Hermitage features a collection of works by Japanese authors of the Ukiyo-e period. He set out to introduce people to the art of that time while inspiring them with exclusive pieces from one of the country's most famous museums. The embossed packaging is anything but accidental, referencing the engraving technique that embodies Ukiyo-e.

DESIGN
Vsevolod Abramov

CLIENT
Okasi

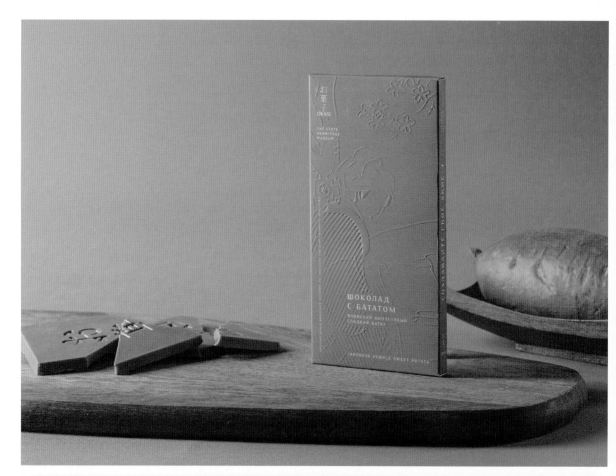

HOLD THAT TIGER BY THE MUDDY BASIN RAMBLERS

The lyrics to 'Hold That Tiger' by The Muddy Basin Ramblers cover an eclectic mix of topics and themes, including folk religions/cults, the East/West cultural divide, the Asian immigrant diaspora in America, the Beat Generation, sci-fi/UFO kitch from the 1950s, and more. To convey them effectively, the kitsch design heavily borrows visual elements from Taiwan's folk culture and Taoist mysticism, as well as a touch of 1950's retro-futurism from the west.

DESIGN
Onion Design Associates

CLIENT
The Muddy Basin Ramblers

146

147

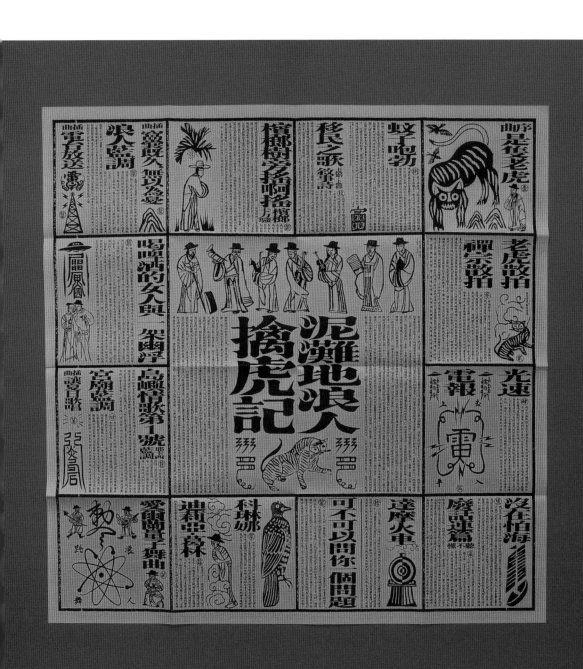

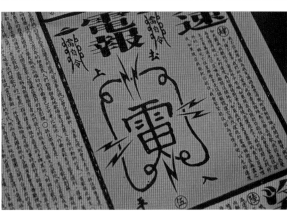

TASTE OF CHINESE ART

As if drinking from a blue-and-white ink painting, 'The Taste of Chinese Art' is a coffee brand that renders an oriental aesthetic through recreating illustrations on glazed porcelain from the Ming Dynasty. The work aims to compare the art of sipping coffee to admiring a beautiful ink painting, where sweet aromas and rich flavours are revealed slowly.

DESIGN
Lung-Hao Chiang

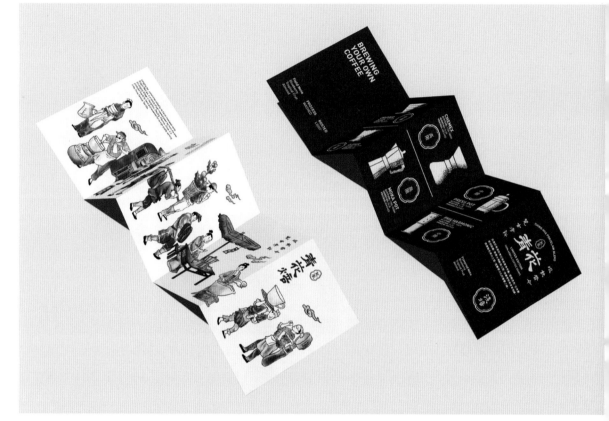

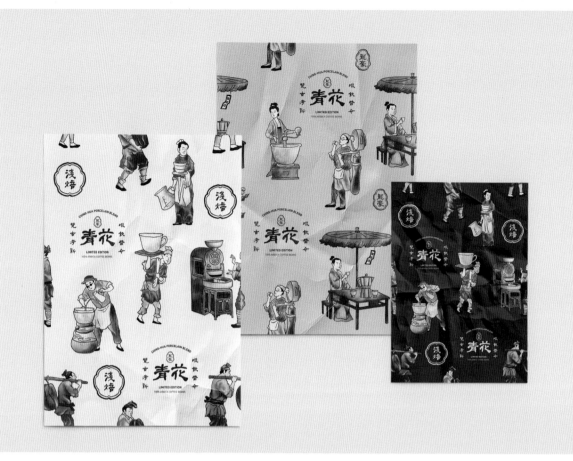

153

DRIP CAFE

BUT. ART PRESENT

DESIGN
ZISHI

PHOTOGRAPHY
but. we love butter

CLIENT
but. we love butter

but. collaborates with Taiwanese artists to explore contemporary Taiwanese culture. For the 'but. Art Present' cookie project, the artists strived to highlight the characteristics of each cookie while articulating Taiwan's multifaceted cultural layers, such as using Tu Di Gong (the God of Land), the phoenix, dragon dancers, and more to metaphorically depict the complex flavours of the pineapple cookie. Overall, the work reshapes the relationship between the traditional and the modern.

BUDDHA JUMP ALBUM DESIGN

FKWU and Tseng Chienying's packaging design work features a motorised structure to showcase the distinct paintings located on both sides of Buddha Jump's album. On the front, a coral pink background enhances the warmth of the fine-brushwork figure painting, while a fluorescent pink background offsets the paper-cut collage on the back. Through the different shades of pink and printing textures, the design reflects the deep layers inherent in the artist's music.

DESIGN
FKWU & Tseng Chienying

CLIENT
Buddha Jump

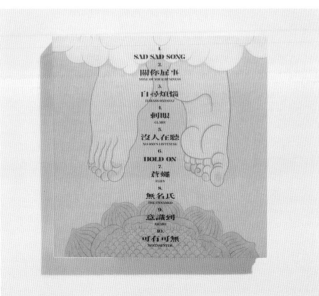

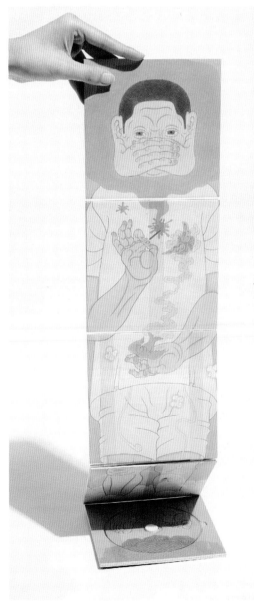

159

160

MELLIFLUOUS

DESIGN
B&A Studio

ILLUSTRATION
Mỹ Linh Pham

Although money is typically given inside red packets during the Lunar New Year as a Vietnamese tradition, B&A Studio wanted to gift something more meaningful. Inspired by traditional fortune-telling sticks and a Đông Hồ folk painting titled 'The Pig Eating Taro Leaves', the studio replaced money with sweet blessings. Besides its trademark ampersand (&) symbol, its red packet design was also embellished with lucky motifs such as gold and firecrackers.

EBISU SUSHI BAR

DESIGN
Youssef El-Sebaei

CLIENT
Nour El-Din Hegazy

Youssef was inspired by ancient Japanese art from the 16th century, including visuals of the god Ebisu, in producing the visual identity for a restaurant in Cairo bearing the same name. One of the seven Gods of Fortune, Ebisu is said to protect fishermen and their livelihoods. Youssef's work features a distinct perspective of modernity to create a simple contrast between nostalgia from the old and the sophistication of the new.

166

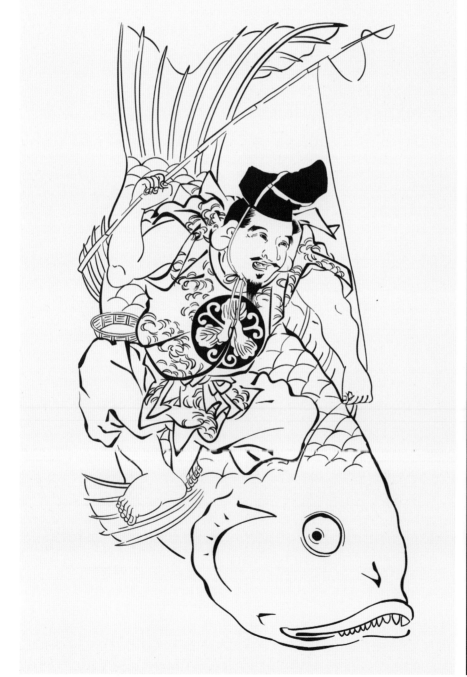

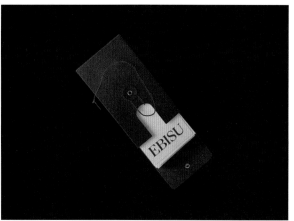

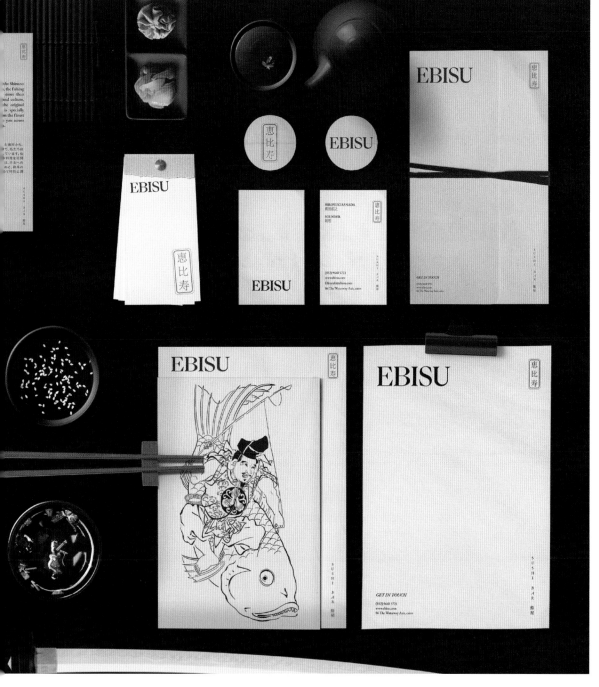

8 IMMORTALS' COLOURS

DESIGN
Where's Gut Studio

Among all the folk art inspired by lore and mythology, an intricately embroidered depiction of 'The Eight Immortals Crossing the Sea' is a popular one that adorns the doors of traditional Chinese households to welcome longevity, happiness, and prosperity. However, lesser known is the old adage behind the tapestry that suggests that the eight immortals each demonstrate a unique prowess – a concept Where's Gut was inspired by in its design.

169

八仙過海
各顯神通

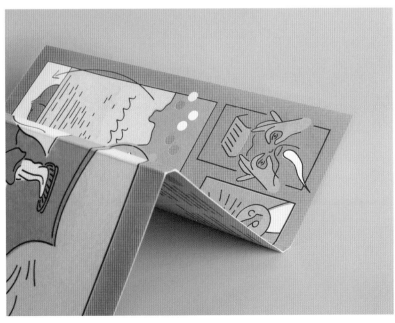

KOLOLAK
HOUSE WINE

DESIGN
Backbone Branding

CLIENT
Messier 53 Hotel Verevan

Kololak or "round shape" in Armenian is a fusion restaurant embodying Armenia's rich cultural heritage. For its house wine collection, the inspiration behind the packaging design by Backbone Branding was Armenian miniatures, manuscripts, and calligraphy – traditional artforms into which the studio infused a distinct contemporary flair. Hand-drawn illustrations featuring famous toasts were also wrapped around the bottle, topped off with a rounded cork to solidify the concept of Kololak.

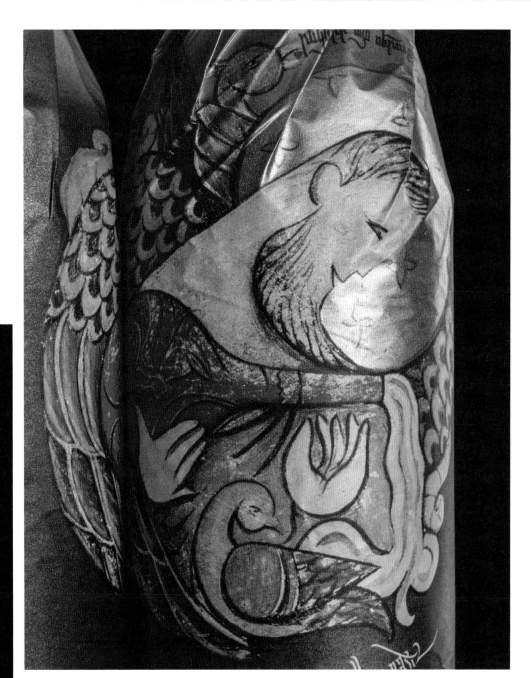

LA BAY LA

DESIGN
DINH QUV TRI THONG

TVPEFACE
DEN by Do Trong Dat

"LA BAY LA" is a personal art exhibition by Thong Dinh, inspired by Vietnam. The name itself can be defined as 'Vietnam of an old acquaintance', through which the artist set out to share his stories and sentiments for his country using the visual arts. To that end, he created a 12-poster collection featuring familiar snippets of daily life in Vietnam through his eyes.

176

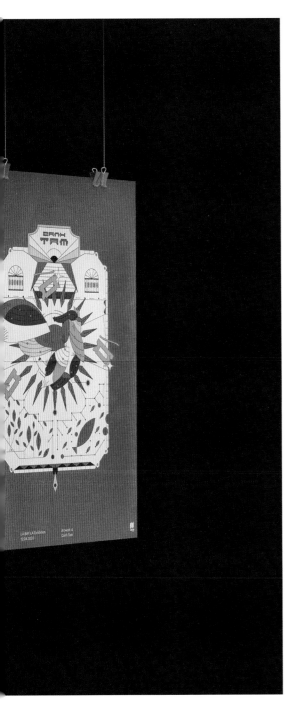

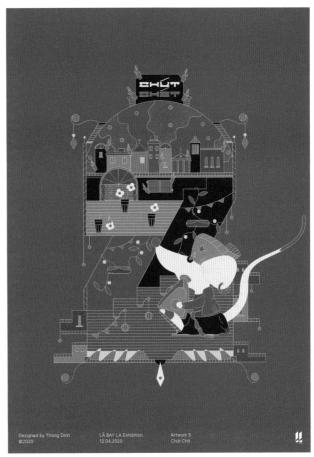

Designed by Thong Dinh
©2020

LÃ BAY LA Exhibition
12.04.2020

Artwork 5
Chút Chit

177

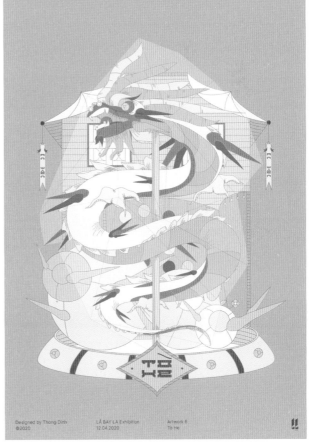

Designed by Thong Dinh
©2020

LÃ BAY LA Exhibition
12.04.2020

Artwork 6
Tò He

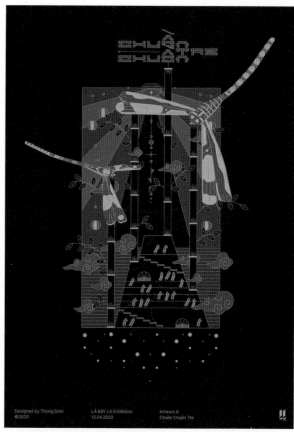

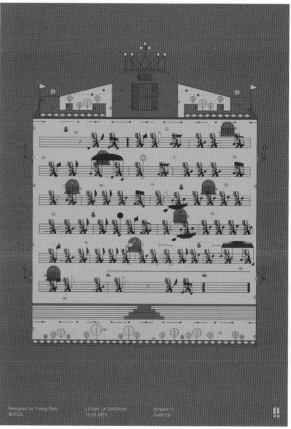

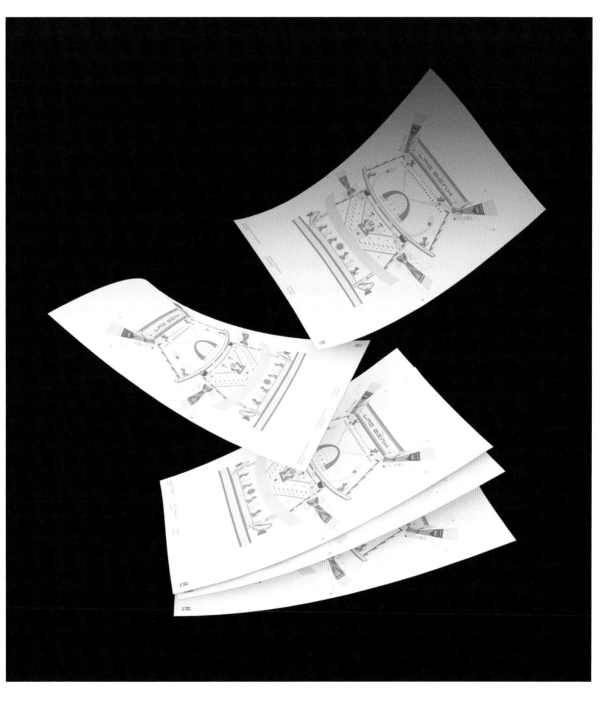

LOCAL SPIRIT WHISKEY

DESIGN
Lung-Hao Chiang

Local Spirit Whiskey is a fun and tasteful reference to the revered deities in Chinese traditional folklore. Using the different aromas such as floral, woody, and smoky to accompany each deity's persona, Lung Hao-Chiang paired herbal notes with the God of Earth, or fruity notes with the God of Mercy. The illustrated god personas are also dressed in modern clothing as an emphasis of fusing the old and new together.

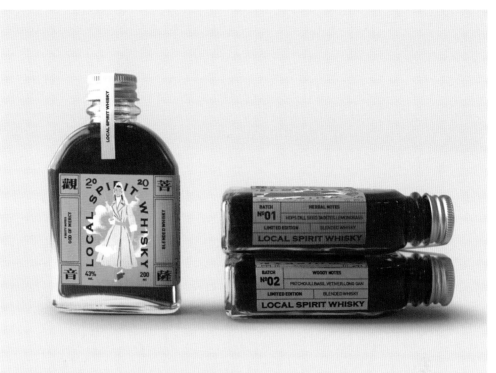

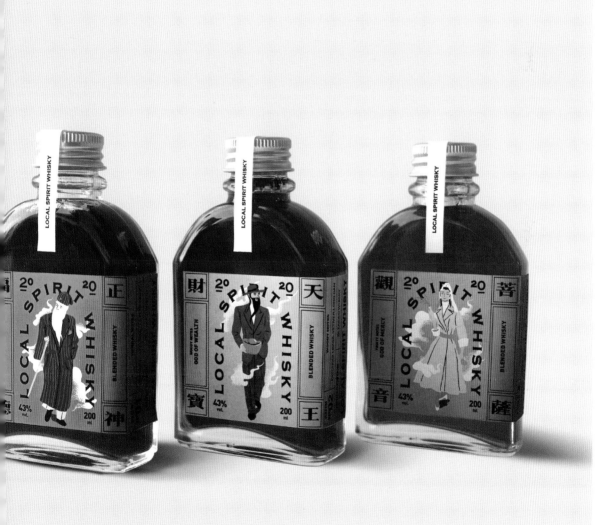

GIÓNG CÀ PHĚ

DESIGN
GM Creative Studio

CLIENT
Gióng Cà Phê

PHOTOGRAPHV
Oanh Phạm

Gióng believes that sincere, heartwarming service has been the cornerstone of Vietnamese culture for generations in fostering sincere connections. To reflect this ethos, the cafe prioritises customer experience by ensuring that every customer need is met in a timely manner. Featuring distinct colours informed by Vietnamese folk art, GM Creative Studio's design work reflects the unique space of cultural experiences in which it resides.

184

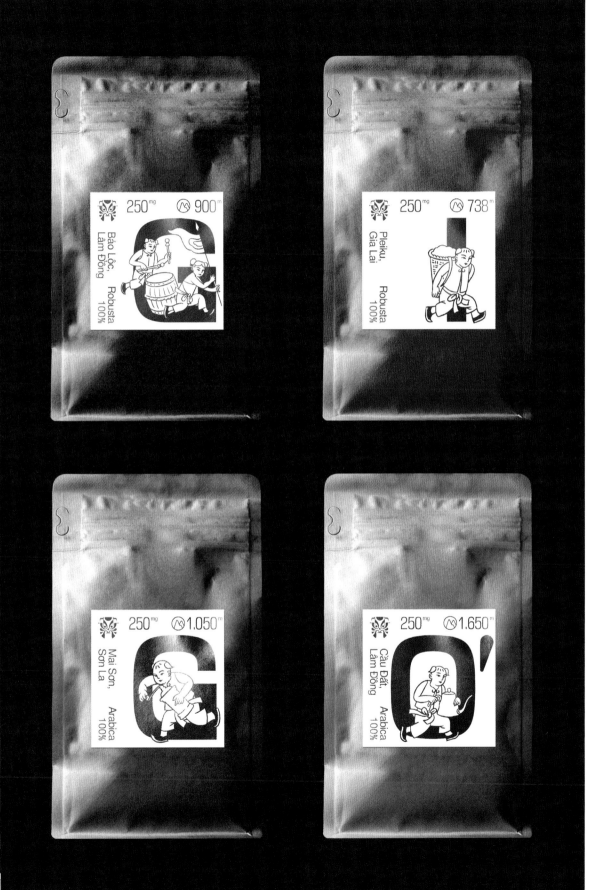

3 FEET

DESIGN
YU-WEI YANG

For "3 Feet", an exhibition named after a Chinese saying inferring that 'a god is always present 3 feet above your head to watch you', Yu-Wei Yang sought to express the idea that even in these modern times, people's lives are still intertwined with the culture of worship. His work served as a starting point for audiences to initiate deeper dialogues on shared cultural beliefs.

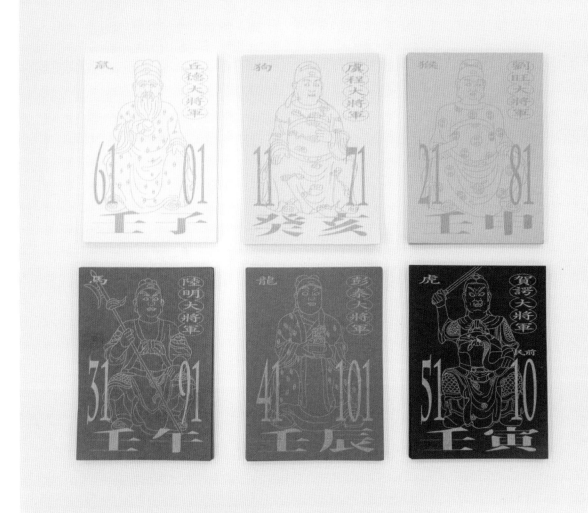

MACAO CLASSIC BRAND

Macao Classic Brand was established by the Macao government to discover and evaluate establishments that embody Macao's unique characteristics, in order to preserve them and support their development into brands of modern significance. Untitled Macao based its design concept on hand-painted advertisements from the old manufacturing/industrial era in Macao, which were iconic of art and design at that time, but reinterpreted using modern design techniques.

DESIGN
Untitled Macao

CLIENT
Macao Economic and Technological
Development Bureau

NMH MUSEUM SKATEBOARD

The NMH Museum skateboard was a collaborative effort between the National Museum of History and ZISHI. The graphic depicts a white elephant and a green lion, symbolising the people's hope for peace and prosperity. According to legend, tamed by Manjushri and Samantabhadra, the animals were regarded as the two bodhisattvas' modes of transportation. This concept was applied to the skateboard, which is a mode of transportation today.

DESIGN
ZISHI

ORGANISER
247 Visual Art

CLIENT
National Museum of History

LIMNOS WINES RETSINA PACKAGING

Retsina is a Greek resinated wine with years of tradition rooted in old-school tavern culture and local grocery stores. In an attempt to recreate its folkloric connotations, Luminous Design Group sought to highlight elements of an almost-theatrical setting that would remind viewers of a past era. It also worked with familiar concepts such as the laterna and the rosary to narrate key moments from retsina's history through design.

DESIGN
Luminous Design Group

CLIENT
Limnos Wines

SINCHAO RICE SHOPPE

Sinchao Rice Shoppe offers modern Taiwanese cuisine within a chic, art deco-inspired dining environment. In aligning its design work with the restaurant's 1930s-influenced decor, ZISHI reinterpreted scenes from the classic Chinese folklore, 'The Eight Immortals Crossing the Sea'. It combined the familiar story with a giant depiction of Chinese fried rice to draw attention to the reinterpretation of the latter dish that the restaurant serves.

DESIGN
ZISHI

BRANDING
IF OFFICE

CLIENT
Sinchao Rice Shoppe

心 潮 飯 店

八 仙 鍋 海

WHY ARE FOLK ART AESTHETICS STILL RELEVANT IN THESE MODERN TIMES?

Folk art is a great reference in modern times, just as our design was inspired by the hand-painted advertisements and layouts that were very popular in the 1960s and 1970s during the old manufacturing/industrial era in Macau. By reviving retro inferences through contemporary interpretations, three different generations can resonate with each other. The comical and humorous illustrated characters in our work also serve to make viewers nostalgic for the past and cherish old stores with historical value.

● Untitled Macao

To me, folk art is a unique form of art that is of the people, for the people, and by the people. It is all about the community, the culture, and the ideas behind it – a pure yet powerful way to express and communicate.

● Kenneth Kuh

The fact that folk art offers various forms of inspiration through material, colour, and historical value continues to make it relevant in this day and age. To be more precise, the combination of traditional aesthetics and modern graphic treatments is the key factor in making folk art as timeless and iconic as it has always been.

● Quang Bao

As a representation of tradition and culture, folk art is a quintessential form of human expression. There is imminence between folk art and respect for the planet; an intimate relationship between people and their habitat. Moreover, it is often art that stems from the heart, informed by natural beauty and pure design. With folk art, there is a deep resonance of authenticity and meaning that transcends history and fires the soul with inspiration.

● A Work of Substance

In every country, folk art not only lives on on paper but also through education, daily life, etc. We cannot deny that folk art plays an important role in people's minds as something they can relate to, and also as a relevant means for expression and communication. It is the connection point between something new and something that lasts.

● DINH QUY TRI THONG

Art expresses a part of culture just as products sell a part of culture. As the act of expressing and selling often move together in the same direction, folk art can be a very effective tool to transmit the values that make a product unique.

● Barcelo Estudio

Folk art is often based on daily life; it is the decoration of everyday objects based on things that are all around us, based on common themes like the seasons, nature, or the circle of life. When I am looking at different folk art from around the world, I see similarities like growing plants, flowers, and animals. These things are very close to being human – and I think folk art is a universal language that will always be relevant.

● Nick Liefhebber

Folk art is closely related to history and development, and has become one of the most important foundations in creation, influencing and inspiring creators and artists through the ages. In addition, those of different generations are able to add the nuances and elements of their time to enrich it. For example, today's red packets are made of various materials with different print finishes. These presentations differentiate the creative work from previous editions, allowing for continuous evolution and innovation.

● beck wong

We are living amid a permanent transition of trends and creativity. Connecting with our origins brings us in touch with our humanity.

● ANAGRAMA

As the world continues to modernise, it is becoming increasingly important to uphold our traditional cultures and roots. The patterns of folk art are very beautiful, and it is my greatest happiness to see these cultures being preserved and promoted around the globe.

● motchutmy

As humans, we are constantly in search of perfection and the only perfect thing that I think exists is nature. Nature was the first visual approach for humans, which is why the representations of the first cultures, rituals, and nature form the essence of folk art.

● Franko Ro

Folk art is a collection of visuals which soothes us, helps us reconnect with nature, and ignites memories – even scents of maternal warmth. It is the collective visual representation of cultures throughout the years by bringing people together and allowing them pause from modern routines. All these elements are and will continue to be relevant to all of us because they speak to our humanity. Our experience in the modern world is becoming more digitised and visually noisier by the minute, and the human element in folk art provides us an opportunity for recollection, for examining the essence of things, and for remembering that despite all technological advancements, we are part of the same ecosystem – binded by its rules yet inspired by its beauty.

● Boo Republic

Throughout the years, the human race has gone through and experienced a lot of different things. As an artist, it is important to me to know the history of art and design, and to refer to the cultural heritage of different periods. I believe that this also nourishes my personal vision in the process.

● Kseniia Shishkova

One could easily find thousands of temples in Taiwan. I believe they are important not only to worshippers, but also to the public as an indispensable part of their daily lives.

● YU-WEI YANG

We believe folk art aesthetics are important because modern society no longer produces or designs similar types of art. More importantly, we all love vintage design and architecture. Their dated elements are often appreciated by a range of high-class buyers and travellers across the globe. For example, travellers of Portugal will always catch a glimpse of our unique tile culture in various walls and buildings around the city.

● M&A CREATIVE AGENCY

In a highly globalised world where western culture is highly homogenised, folk art contributes to enriching the graphic, cultural, and artistic narratives of different countries. The beauty of cultural diversity lies in the preservation and appreciation of the ways with which different people around the world perceive beauty itself. We believe that design can contribute to this noble mission by rescuing and promoting artisanal heritage because, as the German poet and philosopher Goethe once said, 'Culture and art are not the heritage of individual peoples, but a universal heritage.'

● Monotypo Studio

I believe that art originates from the bits and pieces found in our daily lives, and that these elements slowly pile up to form the base of our culture. Using my work as an example, I tried to find the beauty in the smallest and unnoticed things, such as waste paper, or the fruit wrappings that are often thrown away without much thought. By diving into the details of these often overlooked objects, and rearranging these elements to form new meaning, we can find something charming, interesting, and even valuable in them. Just like folk art, these elements allow us to rediscover hidden meanings in our own traditions and strengthen our own cultural identity through a common resonance.

● FKWU & Tseng Chienying

Folk art aesthetics speak about an area and its people, making them rich resources for visual systems since they go deeper and support a storyline. They can be a great source of inspiration if the project allows for it, resulting in unique creations and stories that speak about culture in a relevant way.

● the branding people

We find the reinterpretation of folk art using contemporary concepts interesting, as it is a way of establishing graphic communication between the past and the present.

● HI! ESTUDIO

QUESTION AND ANSWER

Folk art may refer to all forms of visual art that are made in the context of culture. Today, wherever the elements of folk art are used, they can evoke the feeling of nostalgia as they are deeply rooted in the collective consciousness of ordinary people. As a result, they are not just decorative elements, but also a reflection of the cultural life of a community and its modes of expression. Through a unique visual code, all of these cultural characteristics and values can convert a material object, such as an olive oil container, into an attractive and unique piece of design.

● Ioannis Fetanis

Folk art aesthetics, even in our modern times, still exude beauty and uniqueness. In fact, our Korean ancestors did not create their art based on aesthetics alone – they gave various meanings to shapes and patterns to develop logical art, which is also part of modern design. As a result, we believe that there is no meaningless design.

● Tyodi Hyojin Lee

Good folk art is simply timeless. The onus is on us to better appreciate it, understand it, and share it, while being respectful of its origins.

● PUPILA

We as humans are always attracted to stories and mysteries. Folk art contains a lot of narratives, mysterious elements, hidden meanings as well as human hopes and dreams that we constantly look to, love to decrypt, and are inspired by. At a time when we are constantly being bombarded with digital art, NFTs, and AI-powered visuals, we are appreciating the authenticity of folk art more than ever. Still, nothing is relevant or engaging as they are. It is up to us as designers to make them relevant and engaging. We decided to take a break from modern western aesthetics in some of our projects to embrace our traditions. In fact, we have always been aware of the potential of folk art – our work lies in showcasing it in a new light and exposing it to new audiences who are more than ready for something authentic, as they return to their roots.

Folk art is not only a lasting foundation of modern design but also a form of cultural heritage that can inspire you every day. It delivers beautiful stories from the past, invokes curiosity in modern audiences, enriches the customer experience, and makes a product/ brand stand out. To ensure that audiences do not become too familiar or bored, it is up to designers to perceive, study, and upgrade folk art to offer more exciting and innovative takes. It is a meaningful way for us to proudly nurture traditions and embrace cultures.

● Alex Dang

● B&A Studio

The creative process is somewhat complicated, and in my personal opinion, I think that there is nothing that can be compared to original work. Consequently, the creative person or artist must study the past, potentially drawing inspiration from different cultures and folk art to transform it into a new form. Through the development of technology and interdependence of cultures via the internet today, we find that, in a way, we can describe folk art as the interface through which different peoples can look at each other to express the extent of their originality and civilisation.

● Youssef El-Sebaei

We believe folk art and a traditional approach can guide us in defining our future as it is relevant to the people who will live in it.

● Work by \\'

Ranging from wood-carved items, ceramics, and textiles to clay sculptures, origami, and toys, folk craft is often made/done by hand and spans a multitude of forms. Used for practical purposes or as decorative ornaments, the objects serve as vessels of time that will always carry intangible value.

TRADITIONAL DECORATIONS AND HANDICRAFT

CRAFT

DIALOGUE WITH KSENIIA SHISHKOVA

KOTOK PLAYTHINGS

In the Nizhny Novgorod region, the toy-craftsmen industry has been well-known since the XIXth century and is treasured along with the Polkhov-Maidan painting style – recognisable for its bright floral motifs. From its base in a small village within the region, KOTOK Playthings carries on these precious traditions and perpetuates the value of craftsmanship by making beautiful wooden souvenirs of folkcraft in collaboration with talented artisans and artists.

DESIGN
Kseniia Shishkova

GRAPHIC DESIGN & ART DIRECTION
Artem Strizhkov

HEAD TOY MANUFACTURERS
Lev Akulov, Landysh Bakirova

PHOTOGRAPHY
Oleg Savunov, Vera Mishurina, Pavel Krasnyanik, Evdokiya Zamakhina

Q   We noticed that KOTOK Playthings
uses motifs such as the owl, the chick-
adee, as well as the fish, snake, and
bird for their toys. Is there any significant meaning behind these particular
creatures?

A   Animals have been human companions since
ancient times, inhabiting the world of folk
legends and fairy tales. This world accompa-
nies us in childhood and often follows us into
adulthood. Personally, I cannot imagine my
projects without animals in them. For KOTOK,
the animals we feature are familiar to children of any age.

Q What sets KOTOK Playthings apart from other toys? What do you hope your audience takes away from these creations?

A For me, it is an absolute pleasure to know that our colourful and quirky toys are loved both by children and grown-ups. People buy them not only as gifts for kids, but also as decorative objects for interiors.

Q   Besides spinning tops, stacking toys, and whistles, what other toys or objects are you thinking of making next?

A   Currently, we are busy making wooden kinetic mobiles! I am always thinking of new ways to expand our accessories line, and now we have fancy key rings that double as stacking toy pendants – something between a plaything and a fashion item. We also have many, many ideas for possible collaborations in progress!

Q   What part of Russian culture do you like the most? Are there any special festivals or interesting customs that you would like to share with our readers?

A   Classical Russian literature has always been a huge phenomenon. In fact, Russian folklore heritage is so rich in terms of plots with fairies and magical creatures. I am also a big fan of Soviet animation and highly recommend that you check it out!

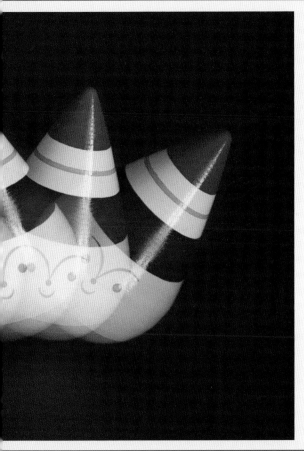

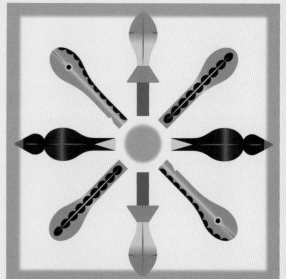

212

2021 CHINESE NEW YEAR RED PACKETS

Harbour City's red packets for Chinese New Year in 2021 aimed to create small moments of joy through their added "foldable-fish" feature. By incorporating origami craft into the design for a 'pop-up' effect, the red packets also became a playful keepsake for recipients young and old. Each set comprised colourful graphics of blossoms to imply prosperity, coins to represent wealth, and a pinwheel to symbolise hope and health.

DESIGN
beck wong

CLIENT
Harbour City

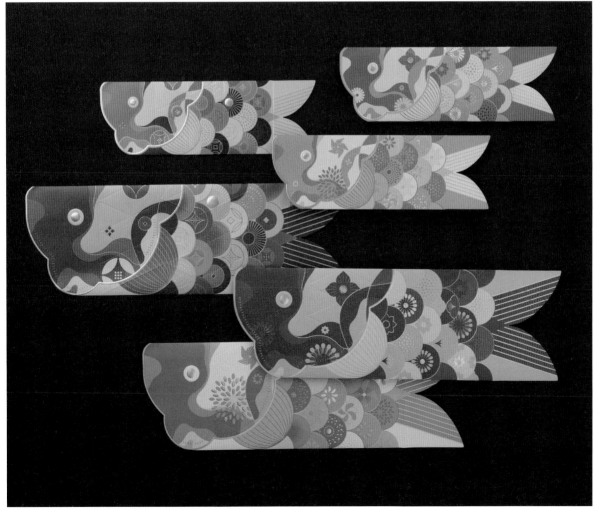

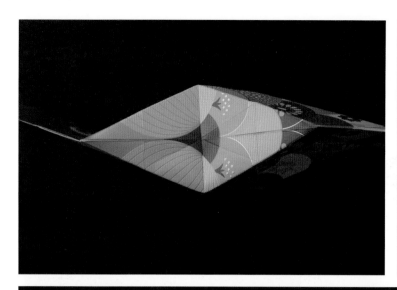

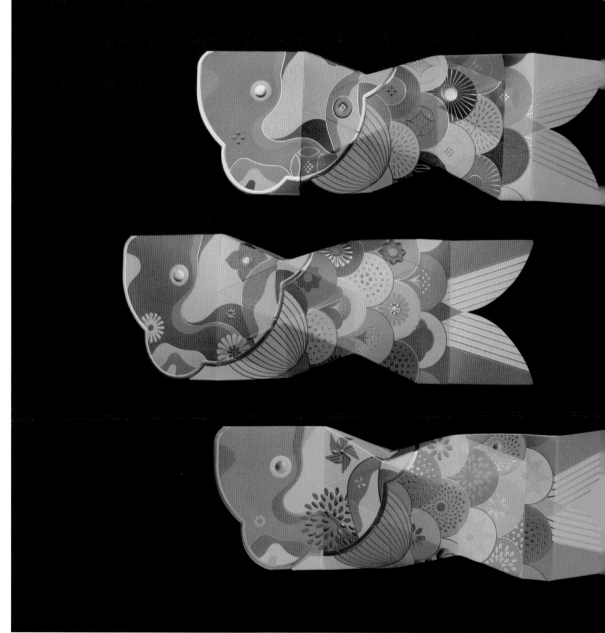

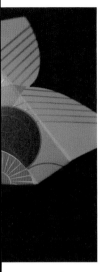

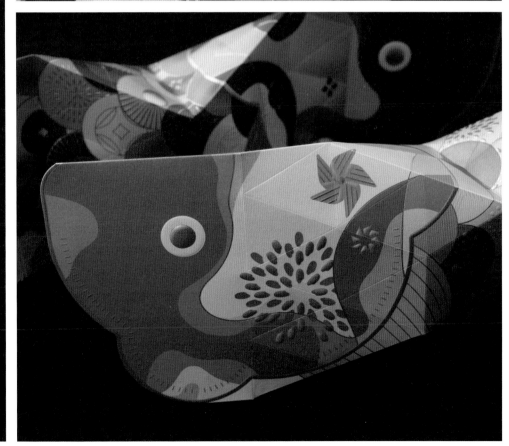

TAPESTRY NEN'KA

DESIGN
RUDA Studio

PHOTOGRAPHY
Marta Syrko,
Anastasia Liubinskaya

MODEL
Mira Bachkur

As part of a project to recover Ukrainian craft techniques and highlight the topic of environmental protection, RUDA Studio created a wall tapestry representing the power and glory of Ukrainian earth. Embellished with the symbol Nen'ka, or Ukrainian for 'mamma', it represents fertility, home guardianship, and power. The handcrafted tapestry illustrates the essential resources of Ukrainian land using different materials, including soil, minerals, wheat, sand, and water.

WARAJI PROJECT

DESIGN
TEKITOJUKU

SPECIAL CREDITS
Palli Crafts Lᵀᴰ,
Chichibu Area Tourism Organization,
seiginomikata, Inc.,
SAKATA BEIKA C⁰Lᵀᴰ

'Ami tumi', or 'me and you' in Bengali, is a new type of upcycled room shoes woven together by Bangladeshi craftsmen using advanced sewing skills and the traditional Japanese craft of 'waraji'. Utilising surplus cloth from sewing factories, the shoes' design take inspiration from local folk designs while creating fair-trade employment opportunities.

218

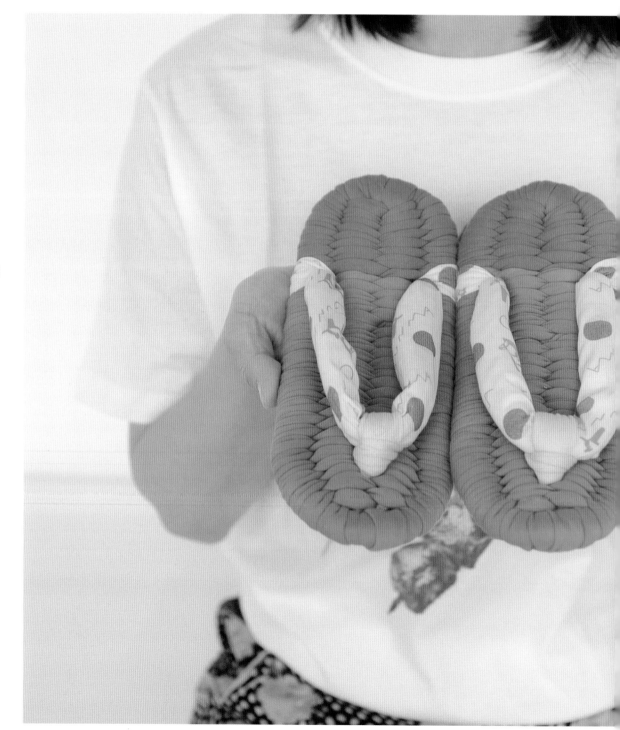

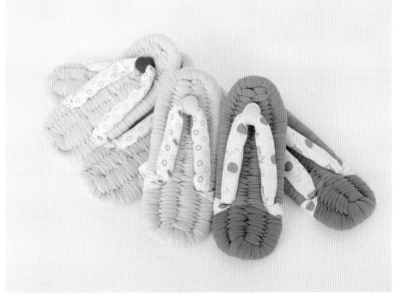

LAND, POGGI UGO 100 YEARS EXHIBITION MILAN DESIGN WEEK

Land is a site-specific installation that celebrates 100 years of Poggi Ugo, one of Italy's most important and ancient furnaces. The project, curated by Valentina Guidi Ottobri, set out to suggest new aesthetic visions of terracotta. In a dialogue of inspiration between the past and present, the project's mission is to work on the idea of travel as revelation, creating a journey that falls back onto Land as a lush and peaceful oasis.

DESIGN
MASQUESPACIO

CURATOR
Valentina Guidi Ottobri

CLIENT
Poggi Ugo

PRODUCER
Poggi Ugo

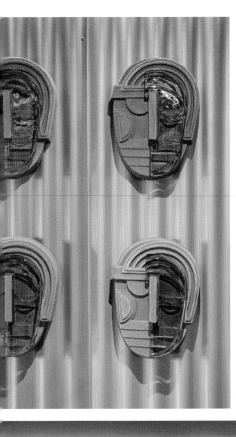

WEAVING TAINAN

DESIGN
VU-WEI VANG

SPECIAL CREDITS
Junmay Label & Textile,
The Place Tainan

The 'Weaving Tainan' exhibition was co-organised by Junmay Label & Textile, one of the biggest jacquard fabric manufacturers in the region, to showcase its weaving technology and craftsmanship through interactive displays and a sensuous tour of the imagination. For the exhibition identity, Yu-Wei Yang reinterpreted traditional symbols to encapsulate the unique beauty of Tainan – based on the idea that like interlacing threads, the ancient and modern are weaved through people.

ASSAI – HANDCRAFTED MODICA CHOCOLATE

For Modica Chocolate's Assai range, Happycentro was deeply inspired by Sicilian traditions to merge the handcrafted chocolate with the classic Opera dei Pupi, a historical representation of legendary poems such as 'Song of Roland' and 'Orlando Furioso' featuring Charlemagne and his paladini. The name 'Assai' itself comes from an adverb commonly used in southern Italy to emphasise when something is "a lot" or "over the top".

DESIGN
Happycentro

CLIENT
Assai

231

GOAT CARD

DESIGN
Gutsulyak.Studio

The idea behind Gutsulyak.Studio's greeting card for the Year of the Green Goat was to focus on symbols and their presence in ordinary things. The card could transform into a mask-shaped decoration that resembled a goat's head. Besides using verdant green vegetation to symbolise a metaphorical paradise, floral ornaments were featured as a tribute to Petrykivka art, which has been added to the UNESCO Intangible Cultural Heritage List.

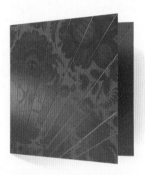

232

LINE OF LIFE PROJECT

The Line of Life Project was initiated by Suntory, a leading Japanese beverage manufacturer that has led many initiatives for environmental and bird conservation across the country. Drawing on the olden days when kites were flown as a prayer to the spirits above, Suntory's endangered storks project in 2015 involved inviting children to fly stork-shaped kites to represent the ties between life and nature.

DESIGN
6D

CLIENT
Suntory

COPYWRITING
Gen Kogusuri

PHOTOGRAPHY
Hiroki Nakashima

MOVIE DIRECTION
Satoshi Takahashi

AGENCY
Toppan Printing

Line of life Project

SUNTORY

237

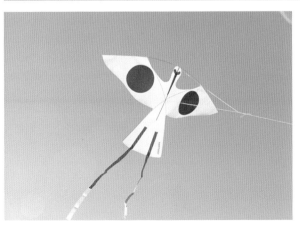

CABINET SOLOMIA

Inspired by the wealth of Ukrainian land and nature, the facades of Cabinet Solomia were encrusted with locally-harvested straw in a traditional Ukrainian technique called solomka. The straw was first cleaned and dyed with natural pigments in RUDA Studio, while the processes of levelling and inlaying were done by hand by local masters instead of machines. The different colour variations of the cabinet represent each time of year, while the natural elements represent Ukraine's fertile land.

DESIGN
RUDA Studio

SPECIAL CREDIT
Anastasia Potapova

DEITY GARMENTS

DESIGN
Vufang Wang

CO-CREATORS
Jasmine Ang, Shao-Chi Lin,
Mei-Ai Wu, Tzu-Vun Lu,
Chia-Ving Lin

The embroidery patterns of the Shinmei or gods' robes are a unique part of Taiwan's traditional arts and temple culture. Although the number of people who understand the value of the embroidery technique is dwindling today, the Deity Garments project aimed to revive it through a set of tools and publications designed to pass on the knowledge to the next generation through educational means.

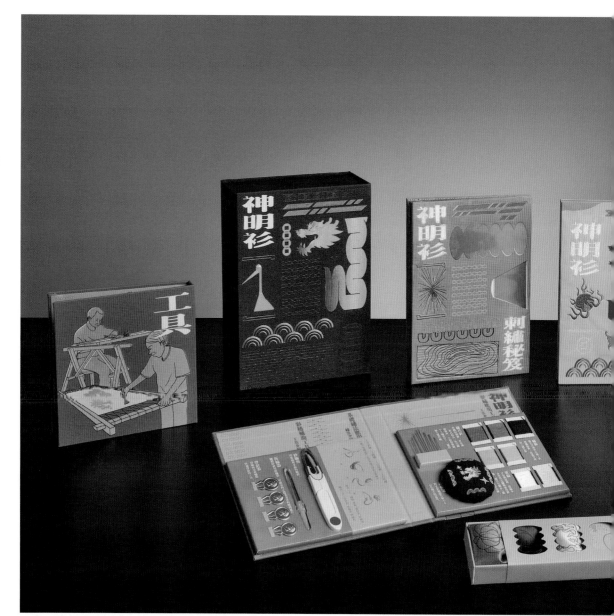

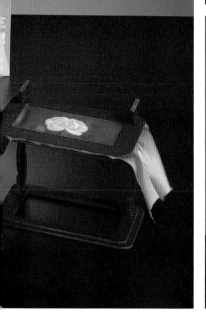

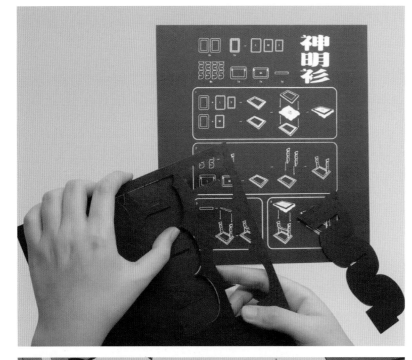

242

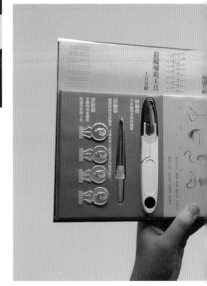

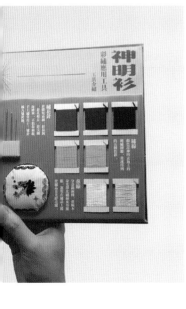

DANGUN PAPER THEATRE

DESIGN
Dasom Vun

Inspired by Buddhist art from the Goryeo dynasty in Korea, Dasom Yun created a series of paper puppets depicting scenarios from the Korean legend of Dangun, the founding myth of Korea that included characters such as a tiger, a bear, and other heavenly deities. The puppets came with a postcard set that could be assembled into a paper theatre backdrop.

244

246

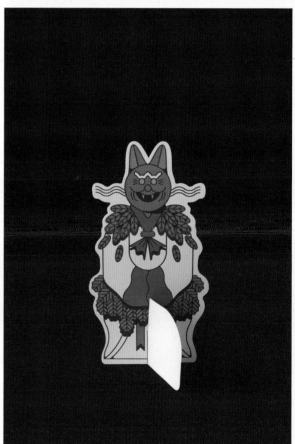

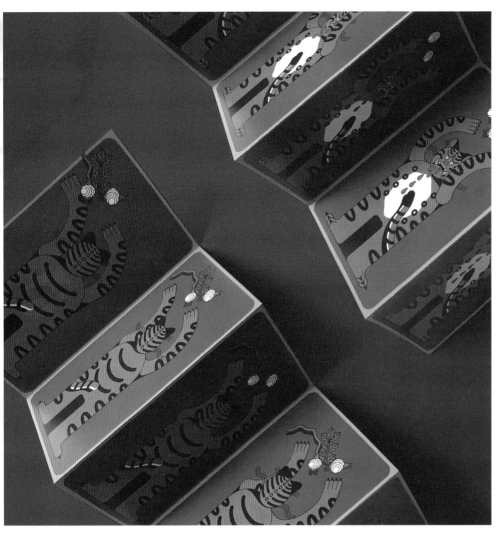

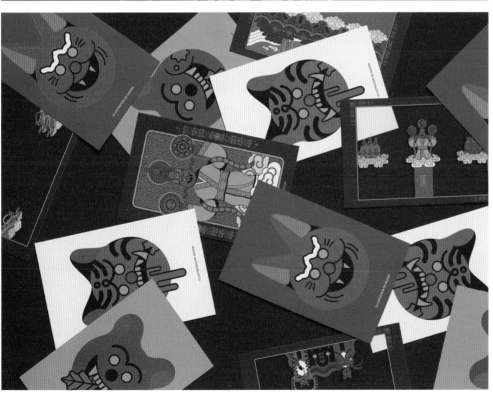

BIOGRAPHY

6D

Shogo Kishino is a Japanese art director and graphic designer who has worked in a wide range of fields including graphic design, CI, VI, signage, and packaging design. Since launching his own design office 6D in 2007, he has won many design awards locally and abroad.

A Work of Substance

A Work of Substance are made of passionate explorers who exercise the art of forgetting what they know and look to maps of the past for vibrant stories about the people and cultures their designs inhabit. In respecting our intrinsic relationship with the environment, they are dedicated to nourishing and strengthening the communities they touch.

Alejandro Gavancho

Originally from Lima, Alejandro Gavancho is an independent design studio in Leeds that specialises in branding, packaging, editorial design, digital communication, and art direction. It defines what it does as a coalescence between powerful aesthetics and real-world applications, working with a strategic, innovative, and international outlook to align brands with human needs.

Alex Dang

Alex Dang is a multidisciplinary designer based in Ho Chi Minh City who collaborates with local and global clients to kickstart their creative journey. Specialising in branding, packaging, editorial design, and art direction, he promotes his concepts via visual experimentation, meticulous craftsmanship, and lots of love.

Amoth studio

Amoth is a Prague-based, award-winning creative studio focusing on branding and packaging design. Founded in 2020 by designer couple Sasha Sharavarau and Tania Sharavarava, it aims to create unique, crafted visuals with stories and meaning behind them, approaching every project with passion, warmth, and care.

ANAGRAMA

ANAGRAMA is an international branding and software development studio specialising in the design of brands, objects, spaces, software, and multimedia. It thrives on breaking the traditional creative agency mould by integrating multidisciplinary teams of creative and business experts.

B&A Studio

B&A Studio comprises a team of creatives that help businesses create agile brands. At B&A, design is both strategic and intuitive; art and science; research and creativity. The studio embraces contrasting ideas and seemingly unrelated disciplines to produce successful outcomes.

Backbone Branding

Backbone Branding is an Armenian independent branding studio and a creative business partner to clients who are ready for extraordinary solutions. The team digs deep into a brand's essence and values – moving beyond design for design's sake to offer consumers solutions that are relevant and incredibly engaging.

Barceló Estudio

Barcelo Estudio is a Palma de Mallorca-based branding and graphic design studio that specialises in creating dynamic brands with flexible systems, packaging, and web design. Its creative solutions are led by a strategic, adaptable, and global approach. Driven by curiosity, passion, and dedication, the team is often involved in characterful local projects that provide social value.

249

250

beck wong

Hong Kong-based beck wong enjoys Chinese typography, print, paper art, and fashion. In 2021, beck co-founded blackhill studio, focusing on fashion design and graphic design.

PP. 213-215

Boo Republic

Boo Republic is a visual communication design studio that provides solutions with aesthetic supremacy and unique character for branding, packaging, and web interfaces. Besides winning at the Red Dot Design Award, Ermis Awards, amd Greed Design & Illustration Awards, its works have been published in The Dieline, Communication Arts, Behance curated galleries, and teaching courses on Domestika.

PP. 10-16, 116-117

Dasom Yun

Dasom Yun is a freelance illustrator based in Seoul who likes to draw detailed illustrations with cheeky characters.

PP. 244-248

DINH QUY TRI THONG

Thong Dinh is a graphic designer and illustrator working in branding/visual identity design and advertising. He is also a teaching assistant at The Fundamental Online. Although he loves working with typography, shapes, and experimental thoughts, he believes that the ultimate art director is always reality.

PP. 176-179

Emi Renzi

Emi Renzi is a graphic designer and illustrator from Casilda. In 2008, he graduated as a graphic designer and moved to Buenos Aires where he trained as an art director and immersed himself fully in the world of packaging and digital art. His work combines diverse elements with colour, texture, and an emphasis on details.

PP. 40-41

FKWU & Tseng Chienying

FKWU is the cofounder of BLOB Studio and a graphic designer who specialises in visual identities for music albums, concerts, exhibitions, and movie posters. He also creates logos for music videos, parties, and concerts on a freelance basis. His collaborator Tseng Chienying is an MFA graduate who loves painting.

PP. 158-161

Franko Ro

Franko Ro is a multidisciplinary visual designer who works as an art director, creative designer, muralist, and occasional taco chef. Currently residing in Amsterdam, he grew up in the city of Tijuana, then moved to Barcelona. He has worked with companies such as Netflix, Puma, ESPN, and Deloitte, to name a few.

PP. 126-127

GM Creative Studio

GM stands for Gao-Muói or 'rice and salt' in Vietnamese. The studio makes ends meet by putting its heart and soul into its work.

PP. 184-187

Gutsulyak.Studio

Yurko Gutsulyak is an accomplished design wizard with over 20 years of mastery in the field. He is the Creative Director and Co-Founder of the award-winning Gutsulyak.Studio. The studio is globally known for its exquisite design focusing on identity and packaging. Gutsulyak's expertise and success has led him to launch the studio in North America and Europe, operating in New York, Toronto, and Kyiv. Gifted with an inventive mind, he has taken part in hundreds of unique projects that have steadily earned him over 150 reputable awards, including European Design Awards, Red Dot, Epica Awards, Pentawards, and Dieline.

PP. 60-61, 232-233

Happycentro

Happycentro is an Italian design, photo, and video workshop comprising professional problem-solvers. Devoted to both the creative and the rational, the group advises brands, plans strategies, designs advertisements, draws storyboards, directs commercials, and creates stop motions. It pushes boundaries, blends disciplines, and experiments with new techniques to tell revolutionary brand stories.

PP. 228-231

HI! ESTUDIO

HI! Estudio believes that the sum of all parts is not the whole, which is why it solves problems by uniting all of its resources in graphic, industrial, and interior design. A multidisciplinary team that believes the most effective way to achieve results is through teamwork, it aspires to accomplish solutions that benefit all.

PP. 84-85

Ioannis Fetanis

Ioannis Fetanis studied at the Athenian Artistic and Technological Group and completed his studies in 2007 by obtaining an MA in Strategic Design & Visual Communication from Middlesex University. Currently, he is a freelance designer who is also active in the social field, such as Creative Action Network and TEDx.

PP. 96-97

Kenneth Kuh

Kenneth Kuh graduated from ArtCenter College of Design in 2020 with a BFA in graphic design and is currently working with Apple. He considers himself a generalist who is constantly challenging the definition of design while looking for the intersection between 2D and 3D worlds, evolving his work across dimensions and axes.

PP. 17-21

Kimbal Estudio

Kimbal Estudio is a Mexican studio that specialises in brand identities and motifs, combining prehispanic culture with contemporary design. Its philosophy is based on a deep analysis and extensive research of the creative concept, thereafter applying the team's multidisciplinary skills to furniture, objects, textiles, architecture, and interior design.

PP. 56-57

Kseniia Shishkova

Designer and illustrator Kseniia Shishkova started the KOTOK Playthings project with her partner in the city of St. Petersburg, where she lives and works on toy design while overseeing the processes of the project.

PP. 206-212

Luminous Design Group

Luminous Design Group is an Athens-based storytelling studio that specialises in identity, print, packaging, and digital design, as well as creative direction. It focuses on designing with a purpose and passion to achieve meaningful, bold, and innovative results.

PP. 198-199

Lung-Hao Chiang

Lung-Hao Chiang loves story-telling via visual and packaging design - especially in the food and beverage industry. He also specialises in product conceptualisation, copywriting, and marketing.

PP. 118-121, 150-153, 180-183

M&A CREATIVE AGENCY

M&A Creative Agency is a multinational, award-winning full-service agency with over 24 years of experience in branding, luxury packaging, and communications. Human-centered and business-focused, it is driven by equal parts creativity, artistry, and innovation. The team combines industrial knowledge with boutique expertise in extending a global reach that forms lasting brand and consumer relationships.

PP. 62-63

Masahiro Minami Design

Masahiro Minami Design specialises in branding, product, graphic, packaging, web, and space design with a focus on promoting local industries and tourism. It analyses its clients' strengths and weaknesses to determine and propose the best solutions.

PP. 77-79

MASQUESPACIO

Masquespacio is an award-winning creative consultancy founded by Ana Milena Hernandez Palacios and Christophe Penasse. Combining interior design and marketing, it customises branding and interior solutions through a unique approach that results in fresh and innovative concepts for clients across the world.

PP. 220-223

251

252

Menta.

Based in Guadalajara and founded in 2008, Menta. is a graphic design studio specialising in brand identities and packaging for hospitality, wellness, and spirits. In celebrating simplicity with a sip of nostalgia, it looks for inspiration in past decades and present times to create meaningful work and human connections by balancing classic and contemporary aesthetics.

PP. 108-111

Monotypo Studio

Monotypo Studio is a design office based in Guadalajara Jalisco which sets out to give its projects a strong visual identity and personality, all while discovering the visual traditions of past generations for today's audiences. From the rationale and concept stages to the final touches, it infuses brands, products and services with a soul.

PP. 26-27, 42-43, 66-68

motchutmy

Hoai My or motchutmy is a full-time graphic designer and freelance illustrator based in Ho Chi Minh City with an affinity for branding, advertising, character design, and traditional beauty, especially in Vietnamese culture.

PP. 98-99

My Creative

My Creative helps brands from all over the world to tell their stories. In creating a successful brand identity with engaging marketing materials, the team joins the dots to not only think about how the brand will look, but also how it could move, develop or even sound.

PP. 100-101

Nastya Lukina

Nastya Lukina is a designer and art director from Moscow who specialises in branding and packaging design. She has worked in leading international branding agencies after studying branding and graphic design at the British Higher School of Art & Design.

PP. 48-49

Nick Liethebber

Nick Liefhebber creates bold, fun and colourful illustrations – both as commissions and for his own screen-/risoprints. Inspired by patterns and rhythms, he uses the associative powers of shape and material to communicate at an intuitive level. His images are built like a collage of paper cuts, ink drawings, and computer-generated imperfections.

PP. 52-53

nju:comunicazione

nju:comunicazione believes in the infectiousness of ideas. Likening its team to a shared brain with multiple intelligences, the studio disassembles and reassembles intuitions to create alternative solutions. In combining experiences and suggestions lifted from many worlds, it is inspired by music, art, cinema, comics, TV shows, and books.

PP. 64-65

NOSIGNER/
Eisuke Tachikawa

NOSIGNER was founded by Eisuke Tachikawa, a design strategist and an associate professor at Keio University who promotes 'Evolution Thinking', a method that helps to generate ideas and inventions by comparing innovation with the evolution of living things to foster game-changers.

PP. 106-107

Onion Design Associates

Onion Design Associates is a multidisciplinary design studio that works in brand identity design and development, art direction, advertising, motion, as well as printed literature. It believes that design should stem from good ideas – no matter how big or small, and seeks to create work that excites, inspires, and most importantly, meets clients' needs.

PP. 146-149

PUPILA

PUPILA is an unconventional design studio in Costa Rica with a love affair for all things brand-related. In 12 years, it has completed over 600 projects around the globe in branding, packaging, editorial design, and more. On top of producing over 50 events across 7 countries, PUPILA has also founded its own coffee brand.

PP. 58-59

Quang Bao

Quang Bao is a Vietnamese designer based in Ho Chi Minh City. He believes that each design project is a combination of various elements with their own history, culture, and civilisation; and that his job is to explore the meaning behind them.

PP. 102-103

RUDA Studio

Oleksandra Rudenko is a designer based in Odesa. After working as an interior and urban designer, she switched to her independent practice of researching object design through nature. In 2017, she founded RUDA Studio together with Yuriy Vovnyanko, which explores and combines Ukrainian traditional craft techniques with the contemporary, and creates products that emphasises on preserving the Earth's natural resources and human interaction with nature.

PP. 216-217, 238-239

Studio Hervik

Founded in 2017 by graphic designer and illustrator Viktor Gkountaras and art historian and museologist Iraklis Gkountaras, Studio Hervik is an independent creative office that offers design, branding, and content services. Experimentation with typography and illustration as well as human-centric elements form the foundation of its creative work.

PP. 104-105

TEKITOJUKU

The Waraji Project was launched by students of Tekitojuku, a Japanese student group aiming to solve social issues with flexible ideas. The students learnt waraji, a traditional weaving technique from Akita, and passed on the knowledge to Bangladeshi craftsmen to create local employment. In 2018, Tekitojuku collaborated with Adobe and various creators to launch Jimoto Waraji, a local event, and exhibited at international events to promote Japanese culture overseas.

PP. 218-219

the branding people

the branding people is a design studio based in Mexico City, specialising in brand construction and visual communications. Through a conscious creative process, the team designs branding assets that assemble eloquence, aesthetics, and functionality.

PP. 132-134

TUKATA

TUKATA® is a Korean lifestyle brand that takes on new perspectives when looking at common, daily objects. Fom those perspectives, it finds and delivers more value to customers. Beyond selling handmade products, it seeks to work towards a happier, more comfortable tomorrow.

PP. 70-76

253

Tyodi Hyojin Lee

Tyodi is a brand experience designer based in Seoul who attempts to deliver differentiated experiences by agonising over various intersections of the brand and its customers. His diverse graphic-and-illustration-based attempts, including branding, are based on things, experiences, and values both old and new.

PP. 112-115

Untitled Macao

Founded in 2017, Untitled Macao is a Macao-based design studio that specialises in infusing design with innovation and unique thinking. Its services encompass brand/visual identity design, event promotion, and signage systems. Over the years, the studio has worked across more than 10 countries and received more than 30 international awards.

PP. 192-193

Voice

Voice gives founder-led, generational organisations a strategy and unique visual presence, helping them build authentic brands that stand the test of time. The team only works with like-minded visionaries who are dedicated to their mission. By combining its clients' powerhouse knowledge with its professional expertise, Voice propels brands to the head of the pack.

PP. 36-39

Vsevolod Abramov

Vsevolod is a graphic designer from Minsk. He began his creative career in small boutique design agencies, going from aspiring designer to creative director. He appreciates a detailed approach to design and pays a lot of attention to typography. He believes that design should help consumers in interactive, mutual, and responsive communication.

PP. 143-145

Where's Gut Studio

Founded in 2018, Where's Gut is a graphic design studio named after the studio cat, Gut, which means both 'luck' and 'tangerine' in Cantonese. Its design practice is based on strategic storytelling to achieve practical solutions that are timeless and engaging by working collaboratively with brands and organisations.

PP. 168-171

Work by \\'

Work by \\' supports businesses by designing meaningful brand experiences through expertly-executed and resonant strategies. It aims to set brands apart from the competition, foster customer affinity to the brand, and help people set the world towards a better course..

PP. 44-47

Youssef El-Sebaei

Youssef El-Sebaei is an Egyptian independent brand designer and concept artist with more than 6 years of experience. He specialises in branding projects by demonstrating his professional expertise in creative strategies. He also enjoys exploring and reinterpreting heritage in a modern way rooted in his passion for type design and illustration.

PP. 166-167

Yufang Wang

Yufang Wang graduated from the China University of Science and Technology in Taiwan and aspires to promote local culture to the world through design.

PP. 240-243

Yu-Wei Yang

Yu-Wei Yang is a Taiwanese designer who focuses on branding, visual identities for events and exhibitions, as well as book design. His collaborator Mark Chen is a graphic designer based in Taiwan who demonstrates his passion in design by immersing himself in a fantastical world and expressing his thoughts through experimental works and out-of-the-box ideas.

PP. 188-191, 224-227

Zilin Yee

Zilin Yee is an Art Director based in Kuala Lumpur, specialising in packaging design and illustrations. Her works are inspired by Asian culture, vibrant colour contrasts and Malaysian batik prints. She has worked with clientele from the Americas and Asia.

PP. 28-31

ZISHI

Founded in 2013, ZISHI is a Taiwanese art and design studio that introduces traditional blue-and-white porcelain aesthetics into modern contexts. Through product design, apparel design, installation and space design, as well as branding, it has created exciting ideas and engaging stories by working with both local brands and international corporations.

PP. 154-157,
194-197, 200-204

ACKNOWLEDGEMENT

We would like to thank all the designers and companies who were involved in the production of this book. This project would not have been accomplished without their significant contribution to its compilation. We would also like to express our gratitude to all the producers for their invaluable opinions and assistance throughout this entire project. Its successful completion owes a great deal to many professionals in the creative industry who have given us precious insights and comments. And to the many others whose names are not credited but have made specific input in this book, we thank you for your continuous support the whole time.

FUTURE EDITIONS

If you wish to participate in viction:ary's future projects and publications, please send your website or portfolio to we@victionary.com